Fathers of a Certain Age

FATHERS OF A CERTAIN AGE

The Joys and Problems of Middle-aged Fatherhood

MARTIN CARNOY

and

DAVID CARNOY

Fairview Press

Minneapolis

Published by Fairview Press, 2450 Riverside Avenue South, Minneapolis, Minnesota 55454.

Library of Congress Cataloging-in-Publication Data
Carnoy, Martin.
        Fathers of a certain age : the joys and problems of middle-aged fatherhood / Martin Carnoy and David Carnoy. — 1st pbk. ed.
                p.   cm.
        Originally published : Boston : Faber and Faber, 1995.
        Includes bibliographical references.
        ISBN 1-57749-031-2 (pbk. : alk. paper)
        1. Fathers—United States—Case studies.   2. Older parents—United States—Case studies.   I. Carnoy, David.   II. Title.
HQ756.C366   1997
306.874'2—dc21   97-612
                                                                                        CIP

First hardcover printing: 1995
First paperback printing: May 1997

Printed in the United States of America
01   00   99   98   97   6   5   4   3   2   1

Cover: Circus Design

Publisher's note: Fairview Press publishes books and other materials on family and community issues. Its publications, including *Fathers of a Certain Age*, do not necessarily reflect the philosophy of Fairview Health System or its treatment programs.

For a free catalog of Fairview Press titles, call toll-free 1-800-544-8207.

. . . .

Contents

Preface vii

1. *Introduction* 1

2. *The Twilight Zone* 13

3. *Honey, I'm Nurturing the Kid!* 37

4. *Older Men and Younger Women* 61

5. *The Adoption Connection* 77

6. *In the Shadows: The Other Children* 97

7. *Eccentric Faddists or Latter-Day Columbuses?* 123

8. *Is Late Fathering Bad for Kids?* 141

9. *Changes* 161

Notes 177

. . . .

Preface

A book about fathering is an emotional undertaking. We the authors are father (Martin) and son (David). Along with David's brother, Jon, we went through a lot together—a painful divorce, living as a threesome for ten years while David and Jon grew into adults and Martin into early middle age, and then major changes again when Martin began a second family a generation after David and Jon were born. When we decided to write together, we knew we were taking a risk. Our own past could have easily prevented us from cooperating, or taking honest criticism from each other, or handling the feelings that arise when you are writing about a subject so close to your own life. But it worked, and more. In discussing and writing about fatherhood in middle age, the two of us, father and adult son, rediscovered our own relationship.

The catalyst for this book was Martin's child of a second marriage—Juliet, now three and a half years old. Here he was, fifty-two years old and a father again. It was a remarkable experience. Fathering seemed so much calmer and more thoughtful the second time around that Martin wondered whether it was just his own reaction or a more general experience. David was interested in the difference between younger fathers his age and what he saw happening between Martin and Juliet. David also wanted to find out how earlier children like him reacted to second-generation families.

We think we answered most of our questions, although we did

not get much help from what others had written. Almost no one has looked at the social phenomenon of fathering after forty-five years old—the group of men we were interested in. We ended up interviewing individuals and using their stories to understand behavior patterns. We did not pretend to be scientific: Our subjects were not randomly selected, we did not use control groups, and we did not analyze our information statistically. We found our middle-aged fathers, their younger wives, and their first- and second-generation children mainly by networking. Because middle-age fathers are so noticeable and the subject of so much discussion among their generational peers, it was easy to find subjects for interviews. We ran into them at parties, on trips, or heard about them from "informants," who shook their heads and marveled at the new fathers' "courage"—or "folly," depending on the informant's point of view. Informants also helped us reach older children and younger wives. All the subjects were well-educated and middle-class, and most were white, again reflecting the nonrandomness of the selection.

Yet we did manage to interview men in a broad range of occupations who live all over the United States. We have disguised the places where our subjects live, and do not use their real names except when they have written about their experiences or been quoted in a newspaper article. We do use the real names of people who are professional psychologists or counselors.

Any book owes much to many. Our greatest gratitude is to the people we interviewed. They gave of their time and were willing to be honest with us to help us understand what older fathering is about. We also want to thank our family, friends, and literary agent, Susan Schorr. They kept encouraging us to do this and to do it together. Of course, we owe a special debt to Betsy Uhrig, our editor at Faber and Faber.

Fathers of a Certain Age

1

. . . .

Introduction

MARTIN: My father was thirty-three when I was born, and my mother, twenty-six. They had met almost ten years earlier, in much better economic times, and married four years after that, but postponed having children because it was the Depression and because, in those days, people like my parents waited to figure out where their lives were going before having kids. My father owned a small advertising agency in Warsaw, Poland, and when the Germans invaded in 1939, my parents, with me in their arms, fled east into what turned out to be the arms of the invading Soviets. Then, in the winter of 1940, we escaped Poland to Lithuania to Latvia to Sweden, and, finally, in July of that year, came to New York City. That's where I grew up in the optimistic 1940s and 1950s. Aside from the fact that my childhood was framed by a war that had annihilated much of my family, my life was pretty ideal. Given the alternative back in Poland, I was always grateful to my parents for having made the moves they did at the beginning of the German occupation.

In those days, my father was about the same age as most other fathers, and behaved about the same. He was in business for himself and worked hard, long hours. My mother played by far the predominant role in raising me. My father would not let her go out and work because he considered her job to be in the home taking care of me and him. In his mind, if she worked, his friends would regard him as a lesser man, incapable of supporting his family. He could not imagine himself doing housework. It was a question of male honor. His honor, defined in the pre–World War I male culture of Eastern Europe,

1

would have been impugned had he had to wash dishes, change diapers, or cook a meal.

My father may have left my upbringing to my mother, but I never doubted the central role I played in his life. He was so busy that I did not do much with him except sometimes on weekends and mainly on vacations. But all our major vacations — until I was in my teens and did not want to go anywhere with my parents — were organized around what they thought I would like. They were usually right. It's almost fifty years ago, but I still remember going fishing with my father on Cape Cod and exotic Algonquin Park, Ontario, where we saw moose and beavers and I caught a smallmouth black bass from a canoe. Those were dream trips for an eight-year-old, and I imagined that my father had created them just for me.

My father lived a long time, and I got to know him pretty well. When we talked, it was mainly about him and his business dealings. As far as I know, that's all he talked about to my two boys — his only grandchildren. When I was in my forties, I came to realize that we never talked about what I did or about us, as father and son. It was not that he was not interested in what I did. To the contrary; he was proud of my accomplishments. He just did not feel it was worth discussing. Neither was he particularly interested in expressing feelings. I think he considered it unmanly. What he did express was his sense of right and wrong — of his honor. Honesty, for example, was a question of honor. Righteousness, which often got him into terrible trouble, was also a question of honor. So was altruism. When we talked about life questions, these were the subjects of our conversations — never what we felt about each other.

When he was in the hospital, just a few months before he died, he told me that I was the best thing that ever happened to him. I told him I loved him a lot and gave him a hug. Even then, he felt uncomfortable talking about such things, but at least we said them. The fact is, though, that these words and the hug were not terribly important. We both knew exactly how much we meant to each other. There was never any doubt in my mind about my father's feeling for me, whether or not he participated in changing my diapers, or wanted to talk about my problems, or whether he took any responsibility for my day-to-day care. He did none of these things, yet he conveyed his intense commitment to me in many other ways. By not ever listening to what my mother and I thought about his decisions, however, he failed in creating the role model that he so much wanted to be for me. Yet, he had an elegance in his approach to life that made me proud and happy that he was my father. When all is said and done, I wish I were more like him, which I guess is the legacy that he really wanted to leave me.

When my first two children were born, I was only twenty-six and twenty-seven, very much in tune with the demographics of the booming sixties. I wanted male children and I got them. I still remember vividly when each was born. I was elated and relieved that they were healthy. I had such fantastic hopes for them. In some ways, my attitudes toward family were like my father's: I didn't particularly want my young wife to work, although I was happy that she was studying toward her Ph.D. My wife and I were also happy to leave the boys — even when they were babies — with their fairly young grandparents, while we went off for two-week vacations. (My parents would occasionally leave me with my grandparents when we lived in Poland). Like my father, I left no question in my children's minds that they were the most important people in my life.

In other ways, however, my family relations appeared to be totally different from my father's. Somehow, between writing books, teaching economics, and demonstrating against the Vietnam War, I changed diapers and was actively involved in my two boys' day-to-day upbringing. Many nights, I cooked for the family, which my father would never have done. Later, I was the boys' soccer coach and took them to hockey practice at six A.M. (My father would not have done that, either.) All this participation was good in some ways and bad in others. It was helpful to my wife and expanded activities for my children, but I began to crowd in on my wife's arena of control at a time when she had little professional life to call her own.

Although I spent much more time than my father did in caring for my children and helping with the housework, my attitude toward my family role was pretty much the same as his. I saw my main obligation as meeting the family's economic needs. We lived well, even though we were very young. We traveled, went skiing, and eventually bought a nice house. My wife only worked at what she wanted to do, and, as far as I was concerned, she did not have to work at all. We always had all the child care we needed to enjoy our lives. But, like my father, at the emotional level I was not really there. I never talked with my wife or children about what I felt or what they felt. I did not consider it important. The difference was that in the late 1960s and early 1970s, that was no longer acceptable behavior. I did not realize that my model for a husband and father was way out of date.

The crisis in my first family came early. My wife and I separated when I was in my mid thirties, after thirteen years of a marriage that I thought would last forever. My and my wife's role models were parents who stayed married forever despite a lot of ups and downs. Divorce just did not fit my career and life plan. But a lot had changed between the 1950s, when my generation's conceptions of love and marriage were formed, and the 1970s, when women took stock of their own lives in marriages and often bailed out. There I was, separated and with two children to take care of. Yes, unusual as it was then and still is, in our joint custody agreement the children were to live with me. Apparently, I was so good at taking care of those family obligations that my wife thought I should maintain primary responsibility. My family crisis also lasted a long time. It took me five years to realize that my wife and I were not going to get back together. During that time, I hung on desperately to the idealistic vision that I had invented for my life, insisting that it would turn out as the great success story I always imagined. Because I had the boys with me, I was far from lonely. And, as I now realize, I turned to my sons for a lot of the emotional support I required. Being a single father did not force me to become a more archetypical nurturing parent, giving love and demanding little back, as one might suppose. Absent my wife and playing true to type, I loved my children but made them take almost as much responsibility for my emotional well-being as I did for theirs.

For better or worse, I waited until my children were grown and in college before entering another permanent relationship. When I did, it was with a woman nine years younger than I who told me that "we were both too old for each other." I was in the midst of a run for Congress, as a Democrat in a fairly safe Republican district, but I was also very excited about this new person I had met. One of the first things Jean and I discussed was children. She did not have any from her previous marriage and did not seem interested in having any, ever. This was the legacy of a big family: At sixteen, Jean had been taking care of a baby sister, the last in a line of nine children. I did not want more children, either. When we moved in together, I, forty-six, and Jean, thirty-seven, looked forward to sharing a politically involved, travel-intensive, childless lifetime with each other.

Somehow, two years later, we were trying to get pregnant. I am not sure how this transformation happened. There was the proverbial "biological clock," of course. But I was in on this; I agreed, even began to encourage. Yes, I realized it was important to her, and she was important to me. Yet I also came to an understanding about myself and children that shocked me: I missed being a father. I am a typical type A and a workaholic, so it was a revelation that I really like children, and that I get as much pleasure from caring for them as from playing power games with my fellow workaholics.

It was too late for Jean to have a child herself, so we adopted — four years later. That is how long everything took: miscarriages, a botched adoption, infertility drugs, and finally a mystical moment in a hospital room with birth mother and brand-new baby. When I first saw her, she was only four hours old, red-faced, with intense, deep blue, just-born eyes that carefully took in my face, the lights on the ceiling, and the emotion-charged atmosphere of the maternity room. After four years of *seeking* refatherhood I had become a father again. My older son was twenty-six, and my younger one had just turned twenty-five. My mother was almost eighty and my father had died two years before. I knew that my life had changed radically at that moment. I also knew that I was extraordinarily happy in a way that went far beyond anything I had ever felt in teaching, writing, publishing, scoring points in debates, or making money. I had had the same rush of happiness a generation before when my first child, David, was born. But the feeling then was also quite different from this time. When I held my son and looked into his blue eyes, I saw myself and family and him as the future. I envisioned his achievements. I was *proud*. This time, when I looked into my daughter's eyes, I saw engagement and involvement. In part, I knew what to expect. I had been through it once before. I knew what parenting meant — the endless demands and enormous responsibility. But it was much more. I began to understand in Juliet's half-open eyes that I had changed. This fatherhood would be less family and achievement for the future than plain old *us* for *now*. By choosing her, I had exchanged twenty years of *me* for twenty years of *us*. As I looked into her eyes, I decided to commit to what all that meant for the rest of my life.

Fathering this time around has been very different. I still work hard. But I also spend a lot of time with my daughter, and, more telling, am much wiser in working out deals that are good for both of us. Yet I also know that I am different, more aware of Juliet *as a child* — not just as an adult-to-be — and of her child's perspective on life. I find myself trying to see things the way she sees them, to sense what she senses. It is a good way to get inside myself. The more I do it, the more I become the pure human being she already is. We trade off: I teach her a moral code and how to survive in a world fraught with danger, and she teaches me to enjoy living. My only fear is that I will stay so enmeshed in the world we adults have constructed that I will fail to learn her lessons well enough.

Is this a good way to spend later middle age and to grow old? Sometimes I'm not sure. Children require a lot of time. But when I let myself get into it, there is nothing better. Is it a good thing for her and my older children that I have chosen to father her so late in my life? Again, I'm not always sure. The main reason I wanted to write this book with one of my sons was to get a sense of the consequences of my act for the others around me.

*

DAVID: My father first told my brother and me that he was thinking of having another child at Christmastime about five years ago. I remember we were in his car, coming back from a shopping center when he announced rather cautiously that he and Jean were thinking of having a baby. He asked us how we felt about it.

His question was met by a long silence. How *did* we feel? My first reaction was shock, then anger. I thought he was crazy. Why would he want another child when he had all these other things he wanted to accomplish? But I have to admit that I was not thinking that much about what it would be like for him. It had just been my brother and me for so long that I couldn't fathom the idea of there being another. And the more I talked, the more upset I got, until I finished by telling him that I was completely opposed to the idea.

My father looked at my brother for help. But Jon, who did not seem to feel strongly one way or another about the news — or just had the good sense to realize that it did no good to be angry about it — didn't say anything. He simply frowned and shrugged his shoulders. Finally, my father said he was sorry we felt that way, and the discussion came to an end.

Why I reacted the way I did is difficult to explain, but I am sure it is tied up with my own childhood and my parents' divorce. When I was about ten years old (and my brother nine), my mother left my father and moved to Los Angeles, ostensibly to become an actress. From that time on, we lived with my father in northern California. We would see our mother once every six to eight weeks — she would either come back up north or we would go down to L.A. for the weekend. But our father was our primary caretaker.

Although this situation seemed unusual to some of our friends, neither my brother nor I found it remarkable. To us, it seemed like the logical outcome of our parents' separation. Dad had always played a very active role in our upbringing. In our early years, he turned us into world travelers, taking us to a new country almost every year. He also encouraged us to play a lot of sports and to excel in them. We were on skis by the time we were three years old, on skates by five, and kicking a soccer ball by six. Outside of school, much of our free time was occupied by sports, and our father was an integral part of that. He pushed us to be the best we could be at everything we did. In a word, he was demanding.

My mother, on the other hand, because of her somewhat rigid upbringing, didn't like the idea of forcing anybody to do anything. She would act as a buffer for us in many situations, telling our father not to demand so much of us. "They're just kids," she would say, "what do you expect from them?"

In the long run, however, my father's voice was just too strong, and he dominated our upbringing. For that reason, it did not seem so odd that we should stay with him instead of going off with our mother when she left. In some sense, his dominance also allowed Mother to leave us without feeling too guilty. On one level, it was her way of saying, Okay, here you go, have it your way, bring them up the way you want. On another level, she knew she was leaving us in capable hands.

For almost four years, there was some question as to whether my parents would get back together. There was talk of us moving down to L.A. and my father becoming a professor at UCLA, but those plans never materialized. I remember hoping during this period that my parents would get back together, but part of me was also resigned to the probability that it would not happen.

I found out they were going to get divorced when I was fourteen. I was looking for an empty envelope on my father's desk when I came across a letter addressed to him from my mother. I had never looked through Father's mail before, but for some reason I decided to read this letter, and, as fate would have it, it was the letter where my parents officially agreed to get divorced.

After I read the letter, I started to cry. It was not the surprise — because it wasn't such a surprise — but suddenly, in those frank words my mother was speaking to my father, the finality of the divorce hit home all at once. There was no denying anymore the fact that they would soon be apart forever.

In the beginning, when they first separated, my father was a little bit lost. For the first year, he really did not date anybody — he was not prepared to — and when he finally did start dating women, he was sensitive to how we felt about the situation. Although Jon and I harbored some resentment toward him for dating, we were at an age (our early to mid teens) when we were beginning to have a healthy curiosity about women ourselves, and we found some of his choices intriguing.

I always had a more difficult time with my mother's boyfriends than with my father's girlfriends. My mother's boyfriends never seemed to be in the same league as Dad. They were not as smart, not as ambitious, and generally not as "with it" as Dad. In short, they never seemed good enough for her — and for the most part, they weren't, and she knew it, which was disappointing to have to watch.

Of course, my father's girlfriends did not measure up to my mother, either, but they came and went quickly enough to keep me from taking them too seriously. They were flavors of the month, little conquests in his newfound bachelorhood. For some reason — I am not sure why — I thought this pattern was going to continue for a while longer. Even after my brother and I left for college, and even after he began having a "serious" relationship with a woman, I didn't foresee my father settling down into the "married life" in the near future. His girlfriend, Jean, was a nice, appealing person, but she didn't stand out from his other girlfriends, so why should things end any differently for her than for the others?

But then, in my senior year of college, Dad called me the day before I was to compete in a major track meet. He announced calmly that he and Jean were getting married in a week. My father's attitude was that it was no big deal, just another marriage.

Well, in fact, it was a bigger deal than he was letting on. He never told Jon or me this, but the reason he got married was that he and Jean wanted to have a child. More than a year after they were married, he suddenly told us in the car that one Christmas, "Jean and I are *thinking* of having a baby, how do you feel about that?" Perhaps a more honest choice of words would have been, "Jean and I are *trying* to have a baby." He did not tell us that Jean had already had two miscarriages.

Obviously, based on my reaction, he had good cause not to be completely up front. I think he knew quite well that we (or at least I) would not be all that happy about his decision to have more children. I think part of him was scared how we would react because he did not want to hurt our feelings or jeopardize our close relationship. But I also think that he felt he did not have to be as sensitive as he once was. We had left the nest, and now he had to do what was right for him whether we liked it or not.

We might have never found out that Jean had lost two babies if it hadn't been for a conversation Jon had with a neighbor one year around Thanksgiving. The neighbor mentioned that she was sorry Jean had lost a baby, causing my brother to blink with surprise. But he never let on that he did not know about it. Instead, he came right home and told me about the conversation. He also called our mother and told her what had happened. She, in turn, called my father and gave him a lecture about how he shouldn't keep things from us.

Father agreed that it was not right, and after that lecture he was more open about what was happening "on the child front." Nevertheless, the episode illustrated how my mother's role in our family had not changed that much over the years.

Just as interesting is how Jon and I have dealt with our father's high expectations as time has passed. My brother never liked the pressure Father put on him, and although Jon is very ambitious — a closet workaholic — he tries to avoid Dad's "lectures," as he calls them. In recent years he has chosen to stay at Mother's house in Los Angeles as his home away from home rather than northern California.

I, on the other hand, have never really minded the pressure my father puts on me, and have, to a certain degree, thrived on it. I have always known that his "lectures" and the pressure he put on us were an expression of his love. And, in recent years, especially after the death of his father, he has been better at expressing his love for us in plainer, simpler language.

At the time I am writing this, I am twenty-nine years old and my brother is twenty-eight. Neither of is exactly what our father (or mother, for that matter) would have liked us to be. Although we are getting better at what we do — I am a writer, my brother a filmmaker — neither of us has had that breakthrough project that will firmly establish us in our chosen fields and provide us with the financial and emotional stability our parents long to see us have. The world, of course, is not the same as it was thirty years ago. Even people with

M.A.'s and Ph.D.'s aren't guaranteed jobs, and even though our parents are aware of that, they still wish we were more settled.

They would also like to see us getting married and having children of our own. Especially in this day of AIDS, most parents would prefer their children to be married and settled than to have them out there risking their lives playing the singles scene. However, neither my brother nor I feel that marriage or children are in our immediate future. It is difficult to predict exactly when we will be ready and it is hardly worth trying to, but what I can say with some definitiveness is that my father's decision to become a father again has taught me a lot about fatherhood and made me feel more prepared to be a good father when my time comes.

By the time his adopted daughter, Juliet, was born, I had become more acclimated to the idea that he was going to have another child. In the long run, I don't know if it would have made a difference whether she was his natural child or not, but in the short run, her being adopted made her arrival easier for me to accept. It meant that my brother and I were still his only true, biological children, preserving what my concept of my family had always been. Almost from day one, my father has tried to get me involved in her life, having me play with her and sometimes baby-sit her when I am in town. One day, when she was about one and a half, he claimed that both he and Jean were sick, and that I was the only one who could take Juliet to "toddler time" at the community center. "She just loves it," he said. "She can't miss it."

Reluctantly, I loaded her in the car and drove off to toddler time. I arrived about fifteen minutes late and when I opened the playroom door, carrying Juliet, all the adults — all of them mothers — looked at me, puzzled. They recognized Juliet, but did not have any idea who I was. Seeing their shock, I quickly announced, "I'm the older brother — the much older brother."

Their looks of puzzlement turned to smiles. Spending an hour with these fifteen mothers and their toddlers was an enlightening and strangely enjoyable experience. After I loaded Juliet back in the car, gave her her bottle, and took her home, I felt I had accomplished something. I was not sure what, but I knew that it had something to do with being a father.

My father, of course, knew this would happen when he sent me out with her. Looking back on incidents like this, I think of him not as the demanding person he can be, but as someone who wants me to learn from his past mistakes and not make them myself. "Don't make the same mistake I did" is a favorite expression of his. When I was born, he himself was not really prepared to have children, so he would like to see me ready to be a better father than he was.

I also see Juliet resisting my father's achievement drive in the same way that I remember trying to set my own pace, not follow his. The difference this time, though, is that my father is letting her have something to say about it. He is listening to what she is telling him. When she digs in her heels, he lets her win. It tells me that he also is not making the same mistakes he did before. He is following his own advice.

My father said he wanted me to write this book with him because he wanted to have the perspective of the younger generation represented in the interviews. He said he wanted to have another voice in the book, so that it would not be "one-sided." But I don't think that's exactly true. I think he wanted me to write this book with him because it would make me learn and think about fathering in ways that I never would have done on my own. And, like making me take that trip to toddler time, it was a ploy to get me more involved in Juliet's life.

For my part, I'm writing with my father for two reasons. First, because I think he was right in arguing that I can look at the subject from a different perspective, giving the book an added dimension, and second, and just as important, it gives me a chance to write a book with the person who has encouraged me most to be a writer. He himself has been the author or coauthor of more than a score of books. I have never read any of them. This will be the first.

2

. . . .

The Twilight Zone

It is Saturday morning, 6:30 A.M., and a faint light is beginning creep through the blinds of the master bedroom where two figures are sleeping peacefully in their queen-sized bed. Suddenly, we hear the sound of a distant thump, like a large book falling off a shelf, then lighter thumps coming closer, and the creaking of a door hinge. One of the figures in the bed stirs, turning over onto his back. This is Adam, who, somewhere in his confused semi-consciousness, feels a weight on his body and then his head.

"Daddy," a tiny voice says next to his ear, "it's time to get up. It's light out."

Adam groans, his eyes still closed.

"Go back to sleep, honey," he manages to say. "It's nighttime." Then, still without moving, not addressing anyone in particular: "Can't you do something about this? I'm fifty-four years old and there's a child sitting on my head at 6:30 in the morning."

"Come into bed with Mommy and Daddy, Alex," his wife, Ellen, says to the three-year-old. Gleefully, the little boy slides off Adam's head and slips under the covers between his parents. He pulls up against his father's shoulder and gives him a hug. "I love you, Daddy."

Adam says that on mornings like these, he feels like he's living in a lost episode of "The Twilight Zone." He is a member of a fast-growing group of men who are fathering in their late forties, fifties, and even sixties. At a time when they should be basking in the midafternoon sun of lives well lived, these men are raising young children.

13

"There are mornings when I'll wake up—or most likely, get awakened," says Adam, "and I'll say to myself, where the hell am I? And who's this insane person in my body who's doing this? And then I realize, it's me. I'm the insane person."

By the time he's had his morning coffee, that attitude has begun to improve. And by midafternoon — the time he usually takes his son to the park where we interviewed him—he feels quite good about himself and the decision he's made.

"It's funny, but I don't see myself as any older than those guys over there," he tells us, pointing to a couple of men in their early thirties playing with their children nearby. "Sure, at some level I know I look like Alex's grandfather, and sometimes I catch strange looks, but in my mind's eye, I'm no different than they are—just another father in the park. I'll tell you this, though, when I take Alex to a playground during the week after work, I am the only father around. That's when I feel really unusual—Mr. Mom. It's just that I'm not into working as hard anymore, and at this stage of my life, Alex is a lot more rewarding to me than work, even if he does wake me up too early on weekend mornings."

Adam is typical of these fathers "of a certain age." They have always been around, but now there seem to be a lot more of them. They are the grayheads standing in line at the supermarket or the folks you mistake for grandparents at the local nursery school.

Our youth-oriented society has become fascinated with them, and well it should. New York writer Lucinda Franks, herself married to a much older man, said to a Chicago *Tribune* reporter, "There used to be a stigma against older fathers. Once, anyone over forty-five was considered an old father. Now forty-five is considered young."[1] The rapid increase of middle-aged fathers and the growing—and, many would say, inappropriate—interest in fathering relatively late in a man's life, is mainly the result of delayed fertility by many professional women and the rise in the divorce rate. The two factors combine to put older men in a position to marry (or remarry) women younger than themselves, and these marriages are often conditioned on parenting, even if it may already be biologically difficult for the woman to have a child. And even that is changing: Technology has made it much more possible today for older women (and their older husbands) to have children even if the wife is not significantly younger than the husband.

The baby boomer population bulge is hitting middle age with the prospect of living another thirty years. Many in this generation feel a need for new, interesting ways to spend the second half of adult life, and older parenting may be an expression of this need. This trend, combined with deteriorating incomes and job mobility for people in their twenties and a resultant postponement of marriage and child-bearing, and no letup in the divorce rate, raises the question whether today's seemingly eccentric older fathering (and mothering) represents the tip of a larger process of social adaptation to economic and technological change.

It all sounds like fun — older men finding new meaning in life as the world around them creates new possibilities and develops new choices; and women attaining professional success first and then having families, too. But not everyone agrees that it is such a good thing. Those who object see older parents as acting selfishly, against the interest of the children they choose to parent. They do not find the gray-heads with preschoolers cute. For many, if not most, Americans, middle-aged parents are just one more symbol of the decay of traditional values and the growing selfishness that puts misplaced self-satisfaction ahead of the greater social good.

With these conflicting viewpoints as a backdrop, we wanted to know more about middle-aged fathering, how it differs from "normal-aged" fathering, and what it means for men, for children, and for the whole concept of parenting in our changing society.

But when we began talking to psychologists and visiting the library to get information about older fathers, we were surprised by how little there was. Few studies exist comparing father-child relations among fathers of different ages, and when they do make comparisons, men over forty are not included. *New York Times* writer Andrew Yarrow's *Latecomers*, a book about the children of older parents, is full of information on middle-aged fathers, but it comes almost entirely from the point of view of children who are now adults.[2] In one well-known study that appeared in *Fatherhood Today* in 1988, Pamela Daniels and Kathy Weingarten compared men who initiated fathering "early" and "late."[3] The only problem is that the fathers Daniels and Weingarten labeled "late" were men in their early thirties — not our definition of "late." The older fathers whom Corinne Nydegger, recently retired professor of medical anthropology at the University of California, San Francisco, considered in her 1982 study of the relations between middle-class men and their children as *adults* were also almost all thirtysomething when the children were born. In contrast to Yarrow, though, she interviewed both fathers and now adult offspring and made statistical comparisons.[4]

These studies did not tell us much about late-middle-aged dads of young children, but they do show that there are even distinct differences in fathering at twenty-five and thirty-five. Daniels and Weingarten concluded that thirtysomething fathers were more secure economically than younger fathers, had more stable marriages, and invested more time in their children. Nydegger found that men who are mature when they become fathers tend to be more understanding and thoughtful parents and are more likely to have close relations with their children, especially daughters. Her data also show that both sons and daughters of late fathers feel more strongly that their father's approval is important to them.

More recently, in 1994, Ross Parke and Brian Neville reviewed research on changes in the structure of the American family from a fathering perspective.[5] That research shows that children of fathers who were in their thirties when their first child was born feel more appreciated than those with younger fathers, and that older first-time fathers (again, in their thirties) are more interested in parenting, more involved in daily child care, and more likely to have a positive experience as fathers. At the same time, they engage less in physical play and more in intellectual activities, and are more responsive, stimulating, and affectionate with infants than younger fathers.

The most important point Parke and Neville make, though, is that fathering styles may not only differ across age groups, but also have almost certainly changed over historical time. In other words, being the father of a young child in the 1950s or 1960s is not the same as being the father of a young child in the 1990s. With this in mind, we looked back at Yarrow's book, *Latecomers*, and realized that it created a problem in his analysis for today's older fathers. Although he was trying to figure out what happens to children who have older fathers, the "children" he got letters from and interviewed were, in fact, adults, most of whom had been reared by their fathers in the 1940s, 1950s, or 1960s. So, how applicable can their perceptions be to understanding middle-aged fathers in today's family context?

These studies gave us some clues about how older fathers were different from more statistically "normal" younger dads. But we could not conclude much about the pros and cons of middle-aged fatherhood from studies that define "older" as men who begin families in their thirties. Neither could we be very confident that information about middle-aged fathers in earlier eras would tell us much about this same age group fathering in the 1980s and 1990s.

Where to turn? Here was a phenomenon of our times, seemingly of intense interest to the media as well as the general public, but only a few researchers had even begun to approach it. How, in a systematic way, could we learn about fathering in middle age? Are older fathers different from younger fathers? Is middle-aged fathering a quirky form of self-indulgence? A response to changing economics and demographics? Is it a fleeting phenomenon, or is it something more premanent?

HOW MANY OLDER FATHERS?

The first thing we wanted to know was how many grayheaded fathers are out there, and who they are. You do not have to have a Ph.D. to figure out that unless society and human biology change much more radically than they have until now, the number of older fathers and mothers is never going to be huge. Since, even in this era, almost all men marry and begin families by their thirties, a man is not likely to be fathering young children when he is older than forty-five. Furthermore, most older men, even when they remarry, do so with women who themselves are approaching forty, which puts biological limits on the possibilities of fathering children. These limits have been extended by in vitro technology, but the physical, emotional, and financial costs of having children this way are daunting.

It is easy to find the number of "older" mothers because they are connected in census data to their naturally-born children. But estimating the number of fathers of young children is much more complicated. The National Center for Health Statistics in Washington, D.C., reported that in 1980 only 48,000 babies, or 1.5 percent of the births where the father's age was recorded, were born to fathers forty-five or older. In 1991, the figure was 67,000, or almost 2 percent of the births where the father's age was recorded. Some of this percentage increase was certainly due to the fact that the younger, childbearing spouses of fathers who were older than forty-five in 1990 were part of the baby boomer population bulge. But some is due to changing fertility patterns.

These data tell us how many babies are born to older fathers each year, but not how many older men in the population are fathering. To approximate the total number of older men in the population with young children, we had to use United States Census data on family

units. Our base was all men twenty or older living in two-parent or
"male-headed" households with children under six. In 1980, the proportion of these men who were forty-five or older was about 4 percent — 475,000 men nationwide. Assuming some of these men are
male relatives but not the fathers of the children, we conservatively estimate the total number of older fathers at about 350,000. We could
not get similar figures from the 1990 Census because the Census
changed in a way that makes it impossible to link information about
men with information about children. But based on the increasing
birthrates to older men between 1980 and 1991, we guess that the
number of middle-aged fathers in the early 1990s is well over
400,000.

The impression given by the media that there are more of these
men than just a few years ago seems to be right. If the birthrates to
men over forty-five years old are any indication of what is going on,
the number of middle-aged fathers (or "much older fathers," as some
call them) rose by about a third. This means that in the ten years between 1980 and 1990, the number of middle-aged fathers of young
children may have gone up by more than 100,000. Even if fertility
patterns do not continue to change, the number of middle-aged fathers should increase over the next ten years as baby boomers grow
older. The Census Bureau estimates that the absolute number of
women twenty to twenty-nine years old will decrease in the 1990s,
but the number of thirty-five- to thirty-nine-year-olds will continue to
increase rapidly. Many of these "older" women will have children
with men over forty-five.

The Census data also tell us that, on average, families with young
children and older fathers are no better off financially than families
without young children and men of the same age. In 1989, the average household income of families where the father was forty-five to
forty-nine years old and had young children was about $58,000,
about the same as the $60,000 for all married couple families with
men forty-five to forty-nine years old. So middle-aged parenting is a
relatively high-income family phenomenon, but only because middle-
aged couples generally earn more than the average (younger) couple.
We estimated that households with young children headed by men
twenty-five to twenty-nine years old had incomes in 1989 of $39,000,
or $17,000 less than those with fathers twenty years older.

SEARCH FOR METHOD

The obvious place to find out about middle-aged fathering was from the fathers themselves. We described the subjects of our interviews earlier in the preface. We ended up doing in-depth interviews with older fathers and children of older fathers in some cases, both with their first set of children (who were now older) and their second set (who ranged in age from eleven to fifteen years old). We did a separate set of interviews of younger wives of older men.

This method is not perfect, of course. Subjects' earlier life experiences are recalled through the filter of later experiences and interpretation, which tends to bias comparisons of later and earlier fathering, for example. And, like most other studies that use the biographical method, our subjects are not a random sample. Yet, we think that because their stories fell into a limited group of patterns, they gave us a reasonably good understanding of what was going on. We also ran some checks, such as interviewing other family members (i.e., wives and first sets of children) and tried to make sense of our results in light of what professional psychologists and sociologists have found out about the behavior of older men and fathers across all ages.

Before talking to fathers, though, we had to know what we were looking for and the problems we might face in interpreting what they told us. We needed a framework to guide us. The characteristic that separates older from younger fathers is obviously age. We began by studying the research on adult development, and in particular, how men change as they grow older. We wanted to know whether there was something about aging that made middle-aged men different from younger men. And, if there was, how did those differences affect their fathering?

The second material we turned to was the historical study of changes in fathers' roles in the family. As we've stated, fathering in the 1990s is different from fathering in previous eras. Many older fathers are fathering for the second time in a generation, and many see it very differently the second time around. But maybe that change is not between being younger and older, but being a father in the 1990s rather than in the 1960s. After all, much has changed in thirty years. Not only has the relationship between men and women changed, but there also seems to have been an historical shift in the role that a father is supposed to play in the family. We have all heard about the 1990s' "new fathering," wherein a father plays a much more active role in the upbringing of his children, sharing in many of the responsibilities that were once the sacred territory of mothers. But is "new fathering" a reality, and if it is, how did it influence the way these older men father?

The third subject that we needed to know about in looking at older fathers was how their children regarded them. What do a man's older, already grown children think about his having more children with a new wife? And how does his advanced age affect his second, younger set of children as they grow up? Do they think about how he may die before they graduate from college? Are they embarrassed at school when he's mistaken for their grandfather? And do they think he's hopelessly unhip and completely out of touch with their generation?

THE STAGES OF A MAN'S LIFE

In the "All the world's a stage" speech of *As You Like It,* Shakespeare wrote, "And one man in his time plays many parts, / His acts being seven ages." He went on to define those ages, each in just a few now-famous words. Yet Shakespeare's and other writers' insights into the distinct changes that marked the passages of adulthood did not become part of scientific analysis until the twentieth century, and even then, did not attract nearly the amount of scientific inquiry that child development did.

The enormous influence of child-centered theories of adult development meant that it took scientists a long time to focus on the nature of change in adulthood itself. Most psychologists agree that it was Carl Jung who made this break. Jung wed two ideas, one that allowed for major changes in adult behavior due to important cyclical changes that take place in adult life, and a second idea that argued for the importance of external cultural forces, particularly mythology and religion. Jung was able to understand change in adults as a combination of forces—including strong childhood influences, external social influences rooted in the symbols of culture, and the demands of family, community, and jobs—on adults still trying to work out the conflicts of childhood.

Erik Erikson continued this new conception in a different form. He popularized the idea of a life cycle marked by identifiable stages in *Childhood and Society,* published in 1950. Erikson saw these stages as points in life marked by moments of decision. Each moment of decision is necessarily a critical juncture of psychosocial development in a person's life. At each juncture, a person moves forward or back, but in any case is changed. For Erikson, three of the stages are in adult life, and the last is at the end of the midlife decision moment. He did not provide much detail beyond what he believed these stages meant in terms of adult development. The main point we gleaned from reading Erikson is that adults are very different at the end of these stages from what they were earlier, and depending on how they resolved issues at each stage, they are different from each other more or less *intimate* or *isolated*, more or less willing to give of one's own experiences to guide the young, and more or less self-integrated into a post-midlife stage of adulthood.

By the 1970s there was a flourishing empirical literature on changes in midlife and adult development in general. The method used by many researchers during this time was the case history of adult lives. Gail Sheehy's *Passages: Predictable Crises of Adult Life*[6] brought the psychology of adult development into mass and upper-middle-class culture. Sheehy used a large number of retrospective case histories of men and women, basing her method on ongoing research by a group at Yale University headed by social psychologist Daniel Levinson. His group did more intensive biographies of a smaller number of adult men and followed them over a two-year period as they went through the midlife change of age forty to forty-five. The Levinson group published their results in a book called *The Seasons of a Man's Life*,[7] and used them to construct a theory of adult development that is specifically linked to age.

Sheehy and Levinson's studies helped us interpret the differences between older and younger fathers because they so clearly contrast men's perceptions, attitudes, and conflicts in their twenties and thirties, when most men father children, with perceptions, attitudes, and conflicts during and after the midlife crisis of the early forties. The comparison gave us a point of entry beyond the anecdotal information reported by journalists into understanding older fathers' experience with their young children as something different from what fathering is at a younger age.

Levinson's major finding is that life structures are characterized by their relatively orderly evolution through a sequence of predictable stages *at particular ages* in the adult years, and that the essential character of the sequence *is the same for all men, regardless of social class, race, ethnicity, and religion*. This is a very powerful finding. It means that although choices may differ for different men because of their position in the workplace, social structure, or because of their beliefs, they end up facing similar types of choices at about the same age.

Levinson begins the sequence of periods in adult development with Early Adulthood, beginning at about age seventeen with the "early adult transition," and ending at age forty, when the midlife transition begins Middle Adulthood. By about age sixty, this stage gives way to the transition to Late Adulthood.

A man's twenties are a period of entering the adult world and separating from family and childhood. In his thirties he anchors himself in the adult world and realizes his youthful aspirations and goals. In the midlife transition, most men question their lives and attempt to redefine themselves to allow neglected parts of the self to find expression. They try to construct a new structure for their lives that will carry them through the next phase, one in which they are past "youth," past climbing the ladder of rapid attainment, and usually past family formation. For some men, Levinson reports, "middle adulthood is often the fullest and most creative season in the life cycle. They are less tyrannized by the ambitions, passions and illusions of youth . . . more deeply attached to others and yet more separate, more centered in the self."[8] The fifties, then, can be a time of great fulfillment for men who are able to rejuvenate themselves and enrich their lives.

Since, in the various transitions, men are making very different kinds of decisions and going through different emotional developments, their relationships with the people around them—especially their family—must have very different contours in their late twenties from those in their early forties and fifties.

When we read Levinson's and Sheehy's studies of the life cycle, we got strange feelings about our our own futures—a mixture of optimism and depressing inevitability. This was just as true for one of us, a young man at the end of what Levinson calls the Early Adult Transition, as it was for the other, already deep in Middle Adulthood. On the one hand, knowing that we will continue to go through major changes was frightening to both of us, even at our very different stages in life. On the other hand, knowing that these phases exist and that they are marked by certain physical and psychological tendencies was reassuring. There *are* resolutions to that seemingly bottomless crisis. As Sheehy puts it in the last, hopeful, sentences of *Passages*, "The courage to take new steps allows us to let go of each stage with its satisfactions and to find the fresh responses that will release the richness of the next. The power to animate all of life's seasons is a power that resides within us."

These seasons can all be rich, but they are also quite distinct from one another, which suggests that fathering during each would be very different, too. Suppose a man were to become a father in his early twenties (Levinson's Early Adulthood). This is a time when it is both biologically optimal for adults to conceive children and when they are most physically capable of dealing with childbirth and the demands of young children. But psychologically, parenting at twenty-five can be extremely stressful. The incompleteness of the transition to adult life means that many of the issues of separation from family are unresolved. Young men often seek refuge in marriage and fatherhood to find the stability that they missed as children. But instead of creating a stable, secure family setting for their own children, they often reproduce the stresses they suffered. Even if the young father is well grounded, his family is bound to be more financially strained than in his thirties or forties. In part, this is offset by lower lifestyle expectations, but it is still often difficult to carry family responsibilities near the very beginning of a work career. As Levinson puts it:

> A man in his early adulthood needs to form relatively enduring relationships with women as well as men. He also needs to accept the responsibilities and pleasures of parenthood and to live out in some measure both the "masculine" and the "feminine" aspects of the self. . . . Given the fundamental importance of these tasks, it is astonishing that nature's timing is so bad: we must choose a partner and start a family before we quite know what we are doing or how to do it well.[9]

The family relationship is also complicated by competing goals. Young men who father in early adulthood are avidly seeking success in work. Although marriage and a family may be formal symbols for men of entering adult life, and though they may satisfy a deep-seated need for forming a stable sexual partnership and conceiving offspring, it is still in the workplace that men find the most important social affirmation of their worth.

"My family had almost nothing to do with shaping the way I behaved toward them and toward the rest of the world," Burt, forty-eight years old, father of two-year-old John, tells us in the garden of his suburban Maryland home. "Obvious as it seems to me today, in those bygone days I could not accept that I had a fathering side that was different from the side I brought to work. Naturally, if I could not see that, I would never let it be me even when I was fathering."

His eyes blaze with intensity and his words come quickly, as if life does not allow enough time for him to comment on everything he knows is out there. We can only imagine how he was in his late twenties, already the father of three young children and an up-and-coming young political science professor trying to get tenure at Georgetown.

"Was I just an insensitive dullard?" he goes on. "Maybe. But I was also a product of the conditions around me. Younger men in my generation usually fell into making family relations an extension of their supercompetitive work lives. Our wives, many of them professionals in their own right, were the *second* in command of the hierarchical family team. When we men were out of town or recreating with friends, she was allowed to make the decisions. Our children had to be smart, good athletes, and all that we thought people who were our children ought to be. We also did a lot of things with them to make sure they were successful. We fulfilled the fatherly tasks that developed our boys into young men and our girls into young women who could go out there and 'succeed.' The 'best fathers' were expected to carry out these tasks with a vengeance, all the while keeping their mind's eye on things they had to do for their work. Our families were mainly an element in our overall achievement drive. Like it or not, our wives and children were part of the day-to-day competition we engaged in during the primary work part of our lives."

For men in their twenties and early thirties who take their work seriously, Burt's relationship with his family was (and still is) fairly typical. Even in the 1990s, men in Early Adulthood are highly likely to believe that they fulfill their family obligation by being hard-driving, competitive breadwinners and spending some obligatory time with the children.

Men in their thirties tend to have a clearer understanding of these issues and know themselves better than men in their twenties. In the later stages of Early Adulthood, after what is often a transient phase of searching for identity, life purposes, and life work, men are more likely to settle down, see their possibilities and limitations at the workplace more realistically, and value their families more highly. But this "settling" or maturation varies by social class. Far fewer men in the working class go through a complete process of realizing an occupational dream; most end up seeing work mainly as a source of earning wages and their workplace as a locale to interact with other men.

For most younger men, though, success in work outside the family is crucial to their self-definition, and "making it" in a job usually requires long hours and devotion that competes head-on with spending time at home. Professionals have it particularly hard, since it is in the thirties that the ultimate effort is required for super success—or even average achievement.

The penalties of not focusing on work are illustrated by a story Betty Friedan tells in *The Second Stage* about a young executive who refused to accept the extra assignments that would have led to a big promotion because they would have interfered with his childrearing obligations at home.

"We're having another child and I'm committed to sharing the responsibilities at home because my wife's going to law school at night," the young executive explained to his boss, assuring him his family duties would not impair his work performance. "But I'm not taking on any extra work because my family's too important to me."

After the executive left, the boss shook his head, lamenting, "That man isn't going to get very far. Too bad. He was the pick of the litter."[10]

THE CHANGING CONCEPT OF FATHERING

Friedan's story suggests something else: Even younger men may be changing their attitudes toward the primacy of work. Has the value they place on fathering changed so radically in the past thirty years that older fathers' experience of a generation ago is obsolete? If we interviewed young fathers today, would we not find family relationships for men in their twenties and thirties very different from what men went through in the 1960s and even 1970s?

Or look at it another way: Maybe middle-aged men are more concerned about having children and spending time with them because of the new emphasis on "nurturing men," whatever their age. Maybe the main change is not between being younger and older but being a father in the 1990s rather than in the 1960s.

Psychologists have long understood the importance of fathers' involvement in caring for and bringing up children, and at least since the 1920s have called on fathers to spend more time with their families.[11] But it took the confluence of two major changes—one socioeconomic and the other ideological—to produce the "new fatherhood," the reconceptualization of the division of parental responsibilities between mothers and fathers.

The socioeconomic change was the dramatic movement of women into the labor force, first mainly as part-time workers, then increasingly as full-time wage earners sharing the work-time burden equally in the two-parent family. In 1950, just 23 percent of married women with children under six worked for wages; in 1986, more than half were in the labor force.[12] The main source of rising average family income in the 1980s was the increased hours worked by women. At the same time, the proportion of households headed by women rose. This trend also forced women to work more hours, especially since divorced fathers, with their own incomes falling steadily, often did not come forth with court-mandated child support.

Not by accident, the ideological shift as to what men's family role should be came at the same time that men's power to earn a family wage began to decline. The feminist movement of the 1970s pressed for a different conception of fathers' responsibility in the family and for changes in the workplace that would allow fathers to balance their work lives with greater participation in the home. Ultimately, this led to the idea that men would be liberated by getting off the fast track of professional success and allowing themselves to become immersed in the more nurturing possibilities of the family. Feminists argued that the definition of manhood had to be separated from man's success at work and from the breadwinner self-image.[13]

If the countless newspaper and magazine articles on changing family roles are any measure, this new ideology had a real influence on the behavior and expectations of American men. One piece in *USA Today* was headlined, "As 'Mr. Moms,' More Dads No Longer Miss Out / Fathers as Caregivers Gaining Favor" (September 22, 1993). The text showed how fathers such as Larry Wade, a Home Depot employee in Woodstock, Georgia, responded to his daughter's unhappiness in day care by working out an evening shift so that he could stay home with her while his wife continued her teaching job. Wade was quoted as saying, "I'm amazed looking back at what I would have missed." Meanwhile, *Parents* magazine columnist Richard Louv wrote, "The payoff is when I'm fathering I feel more like a man than at any other time. I feel more full and more dimensional." And, indeed, the proportion of preschool children cared for by fathers while mothers work rose to 20 percent in the late 1980s after remaining steady for years at 15 percent.

But the evidence on what the new fatherhood means — beyond a vague desire by men to spend more time with their families and the 5-percent higher child care figures — is much more mixed than the amount of press coverage would have us believe. The *USA Today* article itself noted that unemployment and falling income were key factors raising the time fathers spent caring for children. And working mothers were still usually the ones willing to adjust their work hours to care for their children even in families where fathers were the main care provider. Historian Robert Griswold reports that a 1983 study of white, middle-class Boston families found that working fathers married to working mothers spent only forty-five minutes more each *week* with their kindergarten-age children than did men married to full-time housewives.[14]

When we talked with Jerrold Lee Shapiro, a well-known psychologist and writer specializing in men's issues, he warned us not to give too much weight to the studies showing how little time men spent with their children.[15] "Researchers tend to underestimate the amount of time men spend with their children and consciously or subconsciously degrade the quality of men's activities with their kids," he explains. "In our culture, parenting and motherhood are generally equated. Most women define the father as a helper. I don't know how many men have told me how enraged they got when they were with their kids and somebody came by and said, 'Oh, you're baby-sitting.' And the men would say, 'I'm not baby-sitting, that's my child.'"

It is fair to say, then, that men's *views* about getting involved in child-rearing have definitely changed, and that there has been a growing social expectation that men at least *appear* be more involved. This expectation has often led to an actual increase in the time they spend caring for their children. This created some problems for us in interpreting older fathers' comparisons of their earlier child-rearing experiences with their present-day practices. Their participation in child-care activities today could be more the result of the changing ideology and rhetoric around fatherhood than their age and the attitudes that go along with the middle-age transition. The greater commitment and more active enjoyment they get from fatherhood now may have been just as true for them had they been *young* fathers in the 1990s rather than the 1960s, when most were fathers the first time around. The emphasis in the past twenty years on men's nurturing side probably also influenced these older men to become fathers again. It is definitely more legitimate for men to define themselves as nurturing dads in the 1990s than ever before, especially for men who have already proven themselves successful breadwinners.

Because of the changes over time and our limited discussions with younger fathers, we were careful in using our case studies of middle-aged fathers to argue that they are more participative child-rearers. Some of these older fathers are retired and are clearly in charge of child care, but they are unusual. Typically, older men simply have more time for their children because they tend to work less. They also have much less conflict between time spent at work and at home because they are not trying to get ahead in their jobs, and are much less concerned that failure to work longer hours will cost them a promotion.

Were this changing image of good fathering the only shift taking place in fatherhood patterns over the past two decades, our interest in older fathering would not be nearly as great. But other changes in fathering at younger, "normal" ages may be far more important than feminism's effects on fathers' perceptions of their role in child-rearing—changes that make the older-father phenomenon much more interesting.

So far, we have talked only about the perception and the reality of the time spent by fathers on child care in dual-earner households. Yet, since the early 1970s, when the divorce rate began climbing sharply, young men have increasingly ended up divorcing their spouses and therefore not even living in the same family as their children. Not living with children tends to mean not seeing them and not supporting them.

Seen from this larger social perspective, the "new father" could mean many things: the "nurturing father," sharing in the tasks at home, accessible and responsible for infant and teenager alike; the "weekend father," divorced but with joint custody, trying to provide a role model for his children under difficult, limited conditions; or the "absent father," divorced and disassociated from his children.

David Eggebeen and Peter Uhlenberg estimate that between 1960 and 1980, the number of years adult men spent in families where young children were present decreased sharply and the number of years they spent outside of marriage increased. Most of this increase occurred in the twenty- to twenty-nine-year-old age group.[16] Since the average marriage age continued to rise in the 1980s, this trend has continued. The conception of men's passage into adulthood as closely identified with establishing a family, as envisioned by both Levinson and Sheehy, is changing. With greater difficulties in getting a stable job, twenty- to thirty-year-old males may move even farther from marriage and family in the 1990s.

The other part of the change—men's separation and disengagement from their children—is just as impressive. Fifteen million children in the United States grow up having little contact with their fathers, two-thirds because of divorce, one-third because they have been born out of wedlock. Not only has the divorce rate shot up in the last thirty years, leaving more than 90 percent of children with their mothers, but two out of five of these mothers receive no child support, and the 60 percent who do often get payments erratically. Moreover, divorce usually separates fathers from their children's upbringing, distancing them emotionally, and, in more ways than one, clouding their identities as fathers.

CHILDREN LOOK AT THEIR OLDER FATHERS

The most complicated way to look at older fathers is through the eyes of their children. Yet, most people do judge older fathers mainly in terms of how their age (and untimely death) must have a terrible impact on their children's lives. In his book *Latecomers*, Andrew Yarrow draws on eight hundred responses from children of older parents, about one fourth of whom provide emotional detail both pro and con about relationships with their parents.[17] We found the book fascinating. Children's views of their older parents are full of insights. But they are also so full of contradictions that the book made us realize how misleading it would be for anyone to measure the pros and cons of older parenting just from adult retrospectives on parents.

Yarrow's responses came from two groups of children of older parents. The first consisted of children who had older parents because they were last in a series of children and who, more often than not, were the product of accidental pregnancies. The second group consisted of children who were generally the product of *planned* pregnancies—children who had older parents because their parents (particularly their mothers) had delayed childbearing. As might be expected, the opinions of these two kinds of "latecomers" were different, since they played very different roles in their parents' lives. Many of the most negative comments on older parents in Yarrow's book came from the last-in-line children of large families.

When we talked to Corinne Nydegger about her large survey of fathers and their adult children done in 1982, she told us that she had limited the definition of older to the second group—only those families where the father was in his thirties when his first child was born. "My results turn out favorably for older fathers," she says. "The statistical tests showed that that girls got along significantly better with fathers who were older. In some cases — very athletic boys — the opposite was the case, but for the average boy, the reported relationship did not differ by age of father."[18]

The opinions of Yarrow's latecomers may be biased for an even more complex reason. Most of them seem to have been born in the 1950s and early 1960s. That period happened to be a particularly bad time to have older parents. Why? Because older parents' adulthoods were shaped by the Depression (as many of the latecomers' letters to Yarrow pointed out), making them conservative. Meanwhile, their children were growing up in the affluent, rebellious late 1950s, 1960s, and early 1970s, when youth culture was making a collective effort to break with the past. During those years, most parents in America were also a lot younger — the youngest they have been in this century — so the contrast for a child between his or her older parents and the average-age parents was especially stark.

Children born to older parents in the 1980s and 1990s face a completely different set of social conditions. Although older parents are by definition more culturally conservative than younger parents, the older parents of the late 1980s and 1990s were shaped by the affluence and political radicalism of their passage into adulthood. If anything, they would tend to be more "liberal" in their views than younger parents.

Furthermore, today's average parent of young children is older than parents were thirty years ago. In many communities, going to school with a gray-haired mom or dad is not such a big deal anymore. Even though it is still unusual or may draw comments, there may be two or three kids in the class in the same situation. Also, it is much more likely that the child of older parents is not the last in a long line of kids, but the child of a couple who waited until Dad was in his forties, or is the child of the father's second marriage. Far from being "accidents," these children are "apples of the eye." Under today's conditions, children of older fathers would probably tell much different stories from the ones told by those twenty years older. The difference is not due just to the children's younger age at the time of the interview. These are different times.

The negative effects on children of a sick parent or an untimely death are not, however, mitigated by the times. Neither are the fears in children that an older parent may not be around when they are adults. What we cannot tell from Yarrow's analysis (or anyone else's) is what the *overall* effect is on a child's life when the positive parts of middle-aged fathering—especially for the planned, highly nurtured children of late marriages—are balanced against the threat of an earlier death. From the child's perspective, the morality of older parenting has to be weighed in these terms. When we add the tremendous value that older parents place on wanted children, the morality issue becomes even more complicated.

THE GREAT MORAL DEBATE

"My daughter is an everyday miracle," a friend in his fifties tells us, his whole face smiling. Steve has three grown children, all boys, from his first marriage, and a girl, age two, from his second. He is a lawyer who has dedicated his life to social causes, never made a lot of money, but lives comfortably on Manhattan's trendy Upper West Side. Fighting the "big guys," as he calls them, has left a lot of scars and a layer of cynicism, but the hard outer shell seems more porous now than when we first met him ten years ago. In the meantime, he went through a painful divorce and later married a woman ten years his junior. Laurie had been building her own career, and although she too had been married once before, she did not have time for children and thought she never would. Then she met Steve, and slowly everything changed. After three years together, she created an intimate moment, looked at him with her gray, honest eyes and announced that she wanted a child—with a quiet passion that surprised him (but probably should not have, he admits). At first, he resisted. But in the end, she was too important to him to resist very much.

"You don't take the incredible gift of a child for granted when you are in late middle age," Steve goes on. "The unfolding of life has to be savored—observed carefully, contemplated and understood—when your own mortality confronts you daily in the unforgiving reality of the early morning mirror. My attachment to my daughter also has an immediacy and unconditionality that seems more like what mothers are supposed to feel. I have discovered real parenting skills, the ones I was too busy to work on when I was climbing the so-called ladder of economic and social success."

Steve and others who are fathering second families tend to talk a lot about the difference in feelings and commitment they have this second time around. Steve's sense that his values have changed is confirmed not only by these late-age fathers, but most men in their fifties. By their fifties, men tend to know that there are many things they are simply not going to do professionally; if they are lucky, most men begin looking for other ways to live satisfactory lives. Because of these changes, fathers in their late forties, fifties, and beyond tend to value children as much as their work, and often more. They seem to spend more time with their children than younger fathers. Some have retired from the working world completely and take on roles as stay-at-home parents while their younger wives go to full-time jobs.

But with all the intensity of later fatherhood, the new role is not easy. The self-indulgence of late middle age bumps against the energies of a new life demanding attention. Even if an older father may not be as concerned with competing at work, and much more concerned with discovering his emotions, he often wants to focus on himself, his wife, his children from an earlier marriage, or his grandchildren—all of which can be tough competition against the needs of his still-young child.

Most people would probably agree that fathering children in your fifties is "unnatural," not just because of the obvious contrast in physical stamina between a father in his fifties and one in his twenties. The profoundly negative attitude toward late parenthood emerged when a fifty-nine-year-old British woman gave birth to test-tube twins in January 1994. Much of the medical profession (mostly men) came out against such "toying with nature." The French and Italian governments proposed laws that would ban artificial insemination of post-menopausal women. Was this just a reaction against older *women* having children? We do not think so, even though there is surely a double standard that allows older and even "doddering" old men to father children with much less controversy.

However, the double standard is deceptive. We believe it hides a conviction in the population that both middle-aged women *and* men should be playing middle-aged roles—roles that definitely do not include parenting. It is simply more permissible to voice these convictions when a post-menopausal woman, who has to "trick" nature in order to conceive, has a child. Frank Jones, whose column appears regularly in the Toronto *Star*, expressed a more broadly held view when he stated, "I see no need for a double standard. Because I think men in their 50s, 60s, or even older have no business fathering babies. They are simply confusing their proper and appropriate roles as grandfathers with the role of father, which belongs to men half their age."

One older father, Larry, was talking to the wife of an old friend when the conversation turned abruptly to older parents. The wife, highly educated and otherwise very untraditional, was obviously disturbed by the notion that Larry and other men her husband's age are fathering young children. "Imagine Alan [her son] today, at twenty-seven," she said, quite agitated, "if he had been born to a father in his fifties. Suppose his father had even lived that long, he would be eighty. Could a man eighty years old provide the emotional support that a typical kid like Alan still needs in his twenties? Could that same father at seventy have had any meaningful connection with a teenager? I doubt it. More likely, Alan would now have to be taking care of an old man with serious health problems. I don't think kids in their twenties are ready to do that. They should not have to do it. They should be free to think about themselves. God knows, the ego trip ends soon enough, why make them take on the worry of aging parents when they should be exploring life?

"You can't understand something else," she went on, getting angrier. "Both your parents were at your fiftieth birthday party. You don't know what it is to lose a parent when you are young. I lost my mother when I was twenty-one, and I never got over it. It is devastating and unfair. Sure, it happens even when you are born to young parents like I was. But fathers who start in their fifties stand a good chance of dying before their kids are twenty. You may not like that idea, but it is true. It leaves a tremendous void. Children do not get to understand their parents until they have children of their own. If they lose them before that, they never come to terms with who their parents are. The poor kids of older parents. They are condemned to what I suffered, and I don't envy them."

Larry says the conversation shook him to the core. "Was I irresponsible in having a child so late in life?" he worries. "Do children who have older parents and lose them prematurely suffer a harm that makes the whole enterprise pure self-gratification? I realized that in the decision around this child, neither my wife or I had given much thought to whether I would be alive at seventy-five or what I would be like in my sixties as our then teenager confronted puberty and high school. Our main concerns had been around our own lifestyle and how it would have to change. Since I knew how totally intrusive children were, I was also worried about how a child would affect our already happy relationship built on other assumptions."

But as he thought about it further, Larry realized that having a father at a fiftieth or even thirty-fifth birthday as a normal turn of events is a recent phenomenon. His own father was thirty-three when

Larry's grandfather died a "normal" death at sixty-two, and this grandfather was thirty-four when *his* father died in 1912. Today, if a man reaches fifty, he will, on average, live past eighty. True, there is still a good chance that, if he is an older father, his child will lose him in his or her twenties, at a time when many children are still emotionally and financially dependent on their fathers. But there is an even better chance that the father will be there for the child's wedding and the grandchildren.

Larry also contemplated the quality of the relationship with his young child. The changes that men go through in their forties may make them better fathers to such an extent that when they are older it may help the child face that "premature" death with greater understanding and acceptance. The middle-age transition may also make older men better counselors for rebellious teenagers. Less may be at stake and the wide gap in generations could be an advantage, especially when the father has more time and patience to attend to adolescent insecurities.

When Larry had coffee with his friend and his friend's skeptical wife a few days later, he returned to the subject of older fathering. He mentioned the possibility that he would be able to be a better father to his child than he would have been twenty years earlier, and that this could compensate for an earlier departure. His friend's wife would have none of it. "No amount of good relationship makes it any better if your father dies when you still need him. Children do not know that it was a good relationship until they get older, anyway. Having children when you are in your fifties is just plain selfish."

The next day, Larry sought out a psychologist at the university who studies children of divorce. Although he could not do much about his new fatherhood except live it, Larry needed to respond to the profound self-doubt these criticisms had aroused. He wondered whether he had unwittingly dealt his young child a bad hand, and desperately needed an answer.

"Isn't parenting pretty selfish by its very nature?" he asked the psychologist. "Through the ages, haven't adults had children to satisfy adult needs—to perpetuate the family or clan, or to take care of them when they are old, or to increase family income?"

She answered, "I study children whose parents have split up. The children in these cases are the victims of adult frailties. I am not saying the adults are selfish or that the possibility of divorce means that people should not have children, but the fact is that many of these parents should not have had children. Many parents who do *not* get divorced should never have had children, at least from the children's point of view. Look at the incredible amount of abuse that goes on because of alcoholism or a history of abuse in the parents' families. When they grow up, should abused kids go on and have children?"

"What are you telling me?" Larry asked. "How can people figure out that they will be good parents? How do they know whether they should have kids?"

"I think most people think they will be great parents," she replied. "They love the idea of having children and feel perfectly capable of loving them. Often, they believe that having a child to love will solve their own problems. Of course, it doesn't. And then the child ends up paying. Strictly speaking, before conceiving children, all couples should examine their own lives, their relationship, and their genetical makeup. They should have to take care of children of different ages to see if they like those kinds of responsibilities. On the other hand, if potential parents thought carefully about having children and went through the same kind of preparations they do for other life tasks, many who would make great parents might never have children, and the ones who should not have them might go on ignoring their limitations."

Older parents know that they risk making their children face a father's "early" death. Yet they also know that they can give their child a higher material standard of living, more father time, perhaps a higher quality of the father's time, and probably a more stable marital relationship during the years the father is present.

When we ask Larry about this conundrum, he is still not sure what the right answer is. But he does feel that he has probably spent a lot more time thinking about parenting than younger parents do—certainly more than when he had fathered his first child at the age of twenty-seven. He reasons that if the clear moral answer and the path to psychological well-being is not to have a child, he and his wife would have decided against. Given that margin of moral and psychological ambiguity, Larry seems to have settled, at least in his own mind, that he is doing the right thing.

What does it all add up to? Is it morally wrong to father (or mother) young children at an advanced middle age? Do children lose out in important ways because their parents are older? And do older men lose out as well?

This is what this book aims to figure out.

3

· · · · · · · · · · · · · · ·

Honey, I'm Nurturing the Kid!

Fathering in late middle age is different from what younger men experience.

How could that be? All of us who have children can tell stories about three A.M. feedings, sleepless nights, and changing countless diapers. The stories are almost identical, no matter who tells them. Infants act pretty much the same whoever their parents are. They want love and security, and they bond with Mom and Dad to meet those primary needs, regardless of parents' hair color, weight, height, or age.

Lawrence Kutner, who contributes a regular *New York Times* column called "Parent and Child," writes, "Children pay little attention to the wrinkles and gray hairs that adults scrutinize so carefully. Very young children think that anyone over age 15 is old."[1] Ask children about their parents and they will give you opinions that are surprisingly neutral in terms of their parents' age and appearance — surprising to adults, who are much more concerned with these things when they assess other adults. "Daddy is old," a four-year-old will say, upset by some refusal to his demands. His father is only twenty-nine. A very young adult to us, but not to a preschooler.

Children also pass through fairly well-defined physical and mental stages of development independent of their parents' physical characteristics. They begin to smile, to reach, to grab, to walk, to throw their toys, all at predictable times in their young lives. The "terrible twos" happen to the children of teen-age fathers and middle-aged fathers alike.

Sure, parents can and do influence children's development, and older parents may produce somewhat different behaviors in kids than younger parents. But those differences are not large enough to explain why older fathers have such a different experience with children in comparison to younger men. Young children do not really notice how old their fathers are, so the answer does not lie in children's behavior. It is the fathers who act different when they are older. They see themselves and the world around them differently at various stages in their lives. This makes the fathering experience change with age.

Nineteen-nineties "new man" rhetoric aside, fatherhood is not the primary source of most men's identity. Even when we men have families, we tend to define ourselves mainly in terms of job and male social life (including the whole range of male rituals). This self-definition defines how we *see* our children. When jobs and male rituals are central to our lives, the most satisfying (and legitimate) way for us to see our children is as *progeny*, to be provided for materially, played with for a few hours on a Saturday or Sunday, and displayed at church and family get-togethers.

A character in the Russian film *Everything Is Fine* describes being a Jew as "walking down the street with your family," meaning that to feel complete as a Jew, a man needs to show the world his family and to be seen with them. The man tells this story because, in the anti-Semitic conditions of the Soviet Union and post-Soviet Russia, he has been denied the simple ritualistic "walk," and so cannot complete himself as a Jewish man.

In essentially every culture, having a family is part of the traditional (male) definition of "maleness." Until very recently, a man saw his children mainly as extensions of himself—as descendants who would carry his name and his cultural values into the next generation. A man's "walk down the street with his family" represented a display of such reproductive power, hence evidence of his manhood. This concept of fathering says little or nothing about how men should nurture their children, but it assures the reproduction of culture, at least in traditional male terms.

But under the positive influence of women's voices—so long articulated but only recently heeded—and the not-so-positive influence of the much lower wages and job mobility men command today compared to a generation ago, many of us have reconsidered this limited way of seeing our children and therefore defining ourselves as men. We are much more conscious of what a more "democratic" and "equal" family would be like, including shared housework and shared decision-making. We are also more aware of ourselves as fathers-beyond-provider, and our (still) male-dominated society is more willing to view us that way, too.

A mid-thirties vice president of a software company in Silicon Valley, Dave typifies the man sensitive to this new view of the family. He is involved with his infant daughter, Hillary, in ways his father could never have imagined. There are other big differences between these two generations of men. Dave's wife, Ann—unlike his mother—works. Ann, too, is a corporate executive, although she has cut down to half-time to spend more time with Hillary.

Dave picks up Hillary twice a week from the baby-sitter's house at 5:30, then takes care of her for an hour until Ann comes home. Theirs is a reconstructed family, fashioned indirectly by the rise of feminism, and Dave's attitudes reflect the changes. But his use of time is affected only at the margin. His life still revolves mainly around work.

"I know I come home late," Dave admits. "I have commitments to my company, and they are important to me. Despite that, I think I am bonding with Hillary. Actually, I'm less worried by that than how much more pressure this puts on Ann to take care of things around the house."

Ann is not unhappy about Dave's focus on his work. She respects his desire to create a professional identity outside the family and does not feel he is pushing her into more responsibilities at home than she wants. She also feels that he is a good father and is willing to do as much as she wants him to in sharing child care. She sees a major role in the home for herself, but not necessarily for Dave, whom she expects and wants to be successful in his own career.

Dave is excited about his work and is well paid for it. His potential benefits down the road are even higher. If he views his family participation with any remorse, it is mainly because he has internalized a more feminist ideal of family life, not because he feels torn between an unrewarding job and the joy of child care. On the other hand, many other men in their working prime get little satisfaction from work and would really prefer to spend more time with their families than they can afford to.

But the flight from tradition is going both ways at once. Whereas men such as Dave may be more involved with their children than their fathers were with them and though they may have more democratic relationships with their wives, other men are delaying marriage well into their thirties, and some are forgoing it altogether. Whether happy in a challenging job like Dave's, or gloomy in the face of imminent obsolescence, men in their twenties and thirties, the age when they are most likely to have young children, still generally see child-rearing as outside male identity, and not a comfortable alternative to earning income. Many have lost the need to "walk down the street" with their wife and children, and seek identity in less emotionally demanding rituals. In addition, large numbers of divorced men, who fathered children as young men but did not bond very closely with them before the divorce, have lost emotional touch with their children altogether after being physically separated from them.

We know that our self-definition changes as we age. Men in their thirties are at a different point in their lives from men in their twenties, and men in their fifties are different again. They have made it into adulthood, almost universally come to terms with separating from their own parents, and have passed through a transition that defines them as middle-aged. In Erik Erikson's characterization of this transition, those men who have come to terms with themselves at this age have grown into "generativity." They are able to see themselves as passing knowledge on to the next generation, no longer accumulating it mainly for themselves. They have a broader view of their time and their place in the scheme of things.

Naturally, men who have gone through this transition see their relationship with children differently, too. This is not because children have a mysteriously distinctive reaction to older men. Rather, a coming to terms with themselves makes men in their late forties and fifties more patient, more available to children, and more willing to take responsibility for tasks outside their work world.

A 1993 study done by Chicago psychologist Steve Romm suggests that older men devote more time to their children and develop more intimate ties with them than their fathers did with them. Romm's colleague at the Chicago School of Professional Psychology, Joseph Cullen, found that "refathers"—men who have second families—want to develop stronger ties with their second-time-around children than they did with the children they had as younger men.[2]

One refather, Henry, a teacher at the UCLA School of Medicine, explains why this is so. "Young men have many goals, including establishing themselves at work, their hobbies, their sports, and running after women," he says. "These are the product of natural drives, and raising and nurturing children competes with these other important things they want to do. Some of these goals get less intense as you get older, like establishing yourself in your career or running after women. You also get less aggressive about achieving these goals and become more interested in the nurturing aspect of things."

Henry is a successful reasearch doctor who, at fifty-three, is recently remarried and the father of a six-month-old baby. There is still the sound of New York streets in his voice, along with the mannerisms and assertiveness of a younger man. He continues to play tennis three or four times a week and five years ago started a small biotech company to develop his research in pharmaceuticals. He is hardly giving up his career. But by his own assessment and that of his friends, he is doing all this very differently than he would have at forty.

"I think that there are feminine parts of the male personality," he says. "And as you get older you are willing to acknowledge that there are those sorts of feminine characteristics, like nurturing. You are willing to recognize those aspects of yourself because you have more self-confidence. You do what you like to do more; worry less about what others think about you. Once you get into your forties, you decide that you are the ultimate arbiter of what you should be doing. You are relying less on the outside and more on the inside for the decisions you make about what you do. It's more important to do what pleases you than what pleases others."

But, we ask, men who are self-confident at fifty, weren't they also self-confident at thirty?

"I don't think so," he replies. "It isn't the same. At thirty, I was playing the tough guy, but inside I had real doubts about myself and looked to others for approval. I never made a move without checking it out against a kind of popularity poll. Today, I go at my pace, do what feels right. It's also a lot easier for me to relax and enjoy life. If I have greater successes in my work, okay. If I don't, that's okay, too. I have enough money; one more research finding or one more big grant isn't going to make much difference."

Henry spends much more time with his six-month-old than he spent with his two older children, now in their mid twenties, when they were infants.

"I was working at night then," he tells us, "and going to work every morning. I didn't see much of them. At night, my wife, who was also working, was doing most of the nurturing, so I wouldn't see much of them in the evening either. This time around, I spend a lot more time with my kid. I don't work at night and I don't go in to work in the morning. Some mornings I try writing or doing other business at home, but it isn't easy. I usually end up playing with the kid."

Henry says he often wonders why he didn't do this more the first time around.

"I think it's because I don't have the motivation to work at night now, and that's mixed up with my view of personal satisfaction. I would rather have the personal satisfaction of doing something relaxing instead of getting overly exhausted from a lot of work at night. It seems so logical when I say it that I can't figure out why I was doing the opposite twenty-some years ago. But in those days everything that was not work was an impediment to work. I was always *accomplishing my goals,* and that meant working at home and getting in to work early."

For the young Henry, "relaxing with the kids" was not relaxing because it got in the way of these important accomplishments. But since he has achieved success at work, he doesn't see playing with his son or doing housework as something that keeps him from his work. And, as a result, those duties, which once were chores, have now become enjoyable experiences that have value of their own. "Child-rearing is no longer something I *have* to do," he says, "but something I want to do. And that includes feeding the baby, changing him, and whatever else a parent needs to do to take care of an infant."

Several other second-time-around fathers described to us how they had changed as people and as fathers. One man, remarried seven years after a difficult divorce, says: "I had been a father beginning in my mid twenties. I loved my two boys, born two years apart during the roaring 1960s, and even spent some time with them between my job in television production, going to meetings, and demonstrating against the Vietnam War. I was their Little League coach and took them skiing many weekends. But there was something missing from our family life. Even long afterward, I didn't have a clue as to what it was. I can see now that I was good enough at handling the *obligations* of wife and children, yet would not allow myself to become totally *immersed* in family life. My family had nothing to do with shaping the way I behaved toward them and toward the rest of the world — to really *be* a father, heart and soul. Obvious as it seems to me today, in those bygone days I could not accept that I had a fathering side that was different from the side I brought to work."

The change in outlook came late, two years into a second marriage, and after he turned fifty. "I had pretty much lost the crushing drive to 'make it,' " he explains, clearly not altogether happy that this phase of his life is over. "After a while, you perceive that you are just not going to be the dean or the president of the university, and, more importantly, you realize that you do not *want* to be. You want to work hard, but not always have to think about crushing the opposition. You want to enjoy your job *and* enjoy life."

He looks back and assesses what is fleeting and what lasts, and realizes that he ranked things differently as a younger man. Before he remarried, he knew that his wife might want to have a child, but he put it out of his mind. When she became pregnant, he found himself puzzled that he was actually looking forward to the baby's arrival.

"You go through the pregnancy together," he says, "and you get pretty excited, even if you have doubts—even if you know that you are going to have to give up the lifestyle you've become used to. I got this strange sense of looking at my own life, my work, my values, through the pregnancy. It was not really conscious, but I can look back and see what was happening. Now, I'd rather play with the baby in the morning than do my writing. You don't let go completely, of course. I still feel guilty about not completing a small book that I've been working on for ten years. I haven't touched it in the last year. I used to spend a lot of time reading. Now I don't read as much as I did before, and I miss it."

For refathers especially, having children again is a choice that runs against "normal" behavior at middle age. A choice of this magnitude usually brings with it a responsibility and conscientiousness rarely found in younger men, who have children more as "the thing to do" or as part of a natural completion of adulthood.

We heard this story many times over. Alan, a former sixties activist who owns an art gallery in New York, says, "This new kid gets a hell of a lot more time than my other kids did. Why? I've come to believe that it's a good idea—that it's better for him. I don't know that for a fact, but I think it is. And it's because my consciousness about these things is higher, and it's just plain responsibility. I don't want to glorify responsibility, but he's here because of me and my wife, and he's dependent on us. I also have more time, at least in my own mind. I don't have to worry about a place to live and other aspirations that a young person coming up has to worry about. And finally, when I grew up and my other kids grew up, I had no expectations that the world would be a worse place to live. I had a sort of naive confidence that good things were going to happen, that there was going to be progress. This is not the case any longer, and I worry about that. It leads me to want to give him whatever I can give him that will help him deal with what I think is going to be a terrible adversity. I don't want to make the mistake of shortchanging him in terms of what I can do to prepare for the future."

Alan and other refathers we interviewed are painfully aware that their previous generation of children may envy the time and energy they give their new families. The older children sometimes make unkind comparisons between their fathering then and now. But Alan is one refather who sees his new family as an opportunity to build better relations with his older three children, two of whom now have children of their own. "You can't undo the past," he says. "My older kids face many of the same issues in raising their children as I do with my young one, so we have something important to talk about that is about now, not the past. Besides, these days I have more time for my older kids, too."

The desire to focus on family relations — part of the transition that many men go through in their forties — is not just an inward change of attitude driven by work-life cycles. There are physiological changes, too. The body gradually stops producing as much testosterone, and, as Daniel Levinson points out, a man's physical capacity begins to decline in his late thirties. The body at forty-five cannot do what it could do at forty, and this most conspicuous and unavoidable signpost of aging and mortality is one of the reasons that men (and women) tend to reassess their priorities at this age.

Ideological shifts have also had an influence on men's thinking. In today's more feminized world, it is legitimate for men to allow their nurturing side to emerge. The John Wayne, Rambo, and Arnold Schwarzenegger images are still popular, but so are men with feelings. Even Arnold finds it profitable to play kindergarten cop and pregnant father.

This nurturing side comes out publicly when famous, successful men decide that they "need to spend more time with their families." Joe Gibbs, who lived and breathed football for twelve years as head coach of the Washington Redskins, retired in 1993 with the announcement that he wanted to spend time with his two boys. When Lee Atwater, the lunge-for-the-throat orchestrator of George Bush's 1988 presidential campaign was diagnosed as having a brain tumor, the greatest remorse he felt was to have sacrificed family relations for his career.

Alan, the art gallery owner who spoke earlier about how much time he spends with his new child, sees the distance he has from his earlier family as the result of a mixture of a lack of awareness and lack of involvement. "At the time I was bringing up my older kids," he says, "I would have told you that I was a very good father and very much involved within the limits of my work, but looking back, I was hardly aware of what was happening with my kids. I didn't have anywhere near the understanding of what it takes to raise children as I do now, and I spent very little time doing it. Maybe I'm making the same mistakes as I did before, but at least I am conscious of the child-raising decisions we as a couple are making and am very much a part of them."

Late fathers are not the only ones who perceive that their values have changed with age. The women we spoke to who were in their late thirties and forties and who had young children, were generally, if not universally, convinced that their "mature" husbands were more involved with the family and more willing to help than the younger men they knew who had children.

"My husband is there for me in ways that I could never have counted on from a younger man," says Karen, a Santa Clara, California attorney who gave up her lucrative law practice to become a full-time mom at thirty-nine, mainly because she found a man who was willing to be a full partner in raising children. "I have a cousin who's ten years younger than I am, who's married to a guy her age. He's changed their baby maybe three times in this first year. It's not part of his scheme of things, and I hear the same thing from a lot of younger women."

Karen is in the living room of a Cupertino town house, where twenty members of a group called Late Bloomers—older mothers with young children—meet regularly about problems of common concern: children's health, their own health as they approach menopause, the special problems they confront caring for both aging parents and very young children. Most are professionals who work full time, although some, like Karen, have chosen to give up their careers to become mothers. They are self-conscious about their unusual social position, but they are also proud that they are parenting when many of them thought they had passed the biological and social limit for starting a family.

Other women in the group agree with Karen that their husbands spend a lot of time with the kids and aren't afraid of getting their hands dirty changing diapers.

CHERYL: "I'll come home, and my daughter will be in bed. She's had a bath and she'll have played. My husband's taken care of everything."

GRACE: "I'm working with a woman who's in her late twenties and got pregnant. Her husband says, 'I'll play with him after he's toilet trained. I'm not going to change any of those diapers.' But my husband gets up in the middle of the night and changes diapers. He's involved with everything. I don't know if it's a macho thing for a younger man, or if they don't feel that physical care of children is that important or fun, or maybe it's just that they are kind of immature themselves, and still self-centered."

Andrea, who has been sitting back on the sofa assessing the discussion, now leans forward. "I often think that younger men have this illusion of freedom, although how anyone who knows anything about life believes that they really can have that much freedom is beyond me. Our husbands have worked and worked and worked all their lives, and they know that you really don't get freedom, at least not the kind of freedom that these young guys think they get by avoiding family commitments. Older men don't feel that they are relinquishing anything when they are with the children—they aren't giving up illusions. They are living real lives."

Was it a fair test to ask this group of women to compare the parenting behavior of older and younger men? They are highly aware of themselves as "special," and probably want to believe that they are better parents than their younger counterparts. Asserting that their husbands are more involved fathers than all those younger men still wrapped up in their work lives and illusions of freedom is probably partly self-serving.

But two things about these late mothers gave us confidence that those who made these claims about their husbands' commitment to fathering were not distorting reality. First, not all the Late Bloomers we interviewed agreed that men in their forties spend more time at home. Some admitted candidly that their husbands worked long hours or spend a lot of time on the road. They thought of them as good fathers, but not as any different than the younger ones they knew.

Second, these were women who had gone to high school in the late 1960s and attended college and begun their careers at the height of the feminist movement. Even more than Ann (the executive and mother we met earlier in this chapter), they would choose men who would accept a more democratic relationship in the home, consistent with the expectations they had for themselves as "new women." It's not surprising, then, that their husbands would be changing diapers and putting the child to bed as a part of their fathering role.

OLDER FATHERING AND DIVORCE

Many of the men we talked to who were fathering second families were probably reasonably good fathers in their early adulthood, no matter what they now thought of themselves in that role. But their stories reveal that their relations with both their older and new children were deeply affected by what happened in the first family. Almost all second-time fathers we interviewed had been divorced. If divorce is the medium through which these middle-aged men start over again, their attitudes toward raising young children are conditioned not only by their changing values and views of work, but by the breakup of their previous relationship. If they divorced when their children were still young, it almost always meant leaving behind everyday contact with their first set of kids.

Men who were previously divorced and started new families in middle age are the relatively small proportion who either are willing to "pay the price" of having children again in order to marry a younger woman, or who actually want to have children again, this time in a better marriage. Such older men, unlike many others, choose a new partner who wants to make a family. They could make a much more obvious (and usual) choice: Marry a woman who already has children. Even if her children are teenagers still living at home, she takes most of the responsibility for what she naturally sees as hers. Consciously or not, men who get involved with a woman anywhere near child-bearing age who has never had children are pretty sure to be confronted by the "new family" decision.

For example, Dan, who owns a restaurant in San Francisco, was well aware of the path he was taking when, at the age of fifty-four, and already a grandfather, he fell in love with a woman twenty years his junior. "My girlfriend keeps telling me she's all career and has no interest in having children," he said. "But I know that if we commit ourselves to a permanent relationship, all that could change. My decision about this whole thing has to include my willingness to go the next step."

We found that late-middle-aged men's motivation to accept the responsibility for the "next step" is deeply affected by their past.

Some men liked the earlier experience of being fathers as young adults so much that the failure of a marriage or their wife's death sets them looking for someone who would parent more children with them. But most felt that their earlier fathering experience had been incomplete. They often felt guilty at having "failed" the first time around, or at having missed the relationship they would have liked with their children. Some just wanted to re-create what had been a good first father-child relationship, but this time avoid the mistakes that led to divorce. Divorce defined the breakdown of their first attempt at creating and sustaining a family, but it also gave them a second chance. Rather than disengaging from commitment to family life, these men *re-engaged*. We call this "recovering fatherhood."

Fathers recovering fatherhood are very conscious of the shortcomings in their previous life. In their own minds, they may exaggerate these failures because of guilt associated with divorce and "leaving" their children. But whether exaggerated or not, the events of the past almost guarantee that our late-middle-aged dad is going to try very hard to bond with his new offspring and have a close involvement with their upbringing. Since he is all too aware of the cost of letting his family life disintegrate a second time, he is also going to make fathering a major focus in his life. To suffer at sixty the sickening emptiness and guilt he experienced at thirty-five or forty would be disastrous. No work achievement could offset another identity crisis of that magnitude.

There are milder and more extreme versions of recovery. John, for example, is in milder recovery. He is sixty-five, retired, and the full-time father of a three-year-old adopted son named Darin. John has always loved kids, so he had no qualms about having a child so late in life. Nor does it bother him that today he is a full-time househusband, caring for Darin from the time he comes home from preschool (about two P.M.) until Darin's mother, Helen, comes home from work (about six P.M.).

John and Helen spoke to us about their nontraditional arrangement.

JOHN: "The women who do this all the time are amazing—I'm just worn out by the time my wife comes home. But I've really bonded with Darin in a way that I did not bond with my older son, who's now twenty-nine. In fact, when Darin was a baby, since my wife was working, he would not let her do things for him and insisted that I do them, because he did not see her that much. So I arranged with my wife that she should get up in the middle of the night with him and then he bonded with her. These kids really know everything, even when they can't turn over. They can understand everything."

HELEN: "I work full-time and I'm also going to school at night to get a master's degree. It won't get me any promotion at work, but I think that by the time my boy gets to college, a college degree will be like a high school degree now, so I really want to have the M.A. as an example for him."

JOHN: "My wife is the income earner and I stay home. It's not entirely true, because I bring in a lot of income from my assets, but she goes to her job, is getting more education, and I'm here all the time. It sure is different from the first time around. I was working so hard, even seven days a week, that I hardly spent any time with my son. I was working at my job and I was trying to make extra money by buying some property and I had to manage that, so I didn't have much time for him. It may have been the wrong thing to do, but I felt that I wanted to build up our income so the family would be more secure financially, so that's what I did. My relationship with my older son is just never going to be the same as it is going to be with this one, because I was never so involved with him and so close to him. I'm sorry that's the way it is, but at least I am doing it differently this time around."

HELEN: "I think John must have been a good father, because he is so great with Darin. John is too hard on himself. Darin adores him. He is so close to John that I'm really a second fiddle — when he needs something, it's John he wants. And Randy's [John's twenty-nine-year-old] reaction to Darin has been so positive that I can't imagine John and Randy not having a good relationship before, even though they do fight about stuff. Randy comes out here and brings Darin presents and really likes him."

JOHN: "He's still angry with me about the divorce with his mother and some property that I put in Helen's name that he felt should have gone to him. It didn't make him angry with the boy, just with me. Randy and I did spend a lot of time together after the divorce when he was a teenager. We used to go on these two-week fishing and hunting trips up to northern Ontario and Quebec, and just he and I would go, but the fact that this was later on means that I never established that early bond with him, like I am now with my new son. It makes it very different."

John has turned his world upside down, less from strong feelings of guilt about his earlier fatherhood than from a desire to parent again with a woman he met late in life, and his willingness to do it in a different way. He has completed his role in life as material provider and has now shifted to nurturer. He does not regard his earlier fathering as "bad," just distant in those crucial early years when deep emotional links form between parent and child. This is what he is grabbing at now, and he revels in the new emotions he has discovered by taking primary responsibility for a young child.

DIVORCE AND REMARRIAGE

Divorce can make men want to recover fatherhood even when strong bonds have been formed with children in those early years. Yet, even when the connections are strong, divorce is a wrenching force.

Carl started out as a teacher and school principal in a small town in the Midwest. He married young, but that first marriage lasted only six years. Then he met Donna. It was at one of those local preelection political events where people share strong beliefs and a common cause. They fell in love and decided to live together.

"I wanted more education and so did she," Carl says, "so we went off to Minneapolis, to the University of Minnesota, and became graduate students. It was a great part of my life—maybe the best. Somewhere along the way we got married, and Dennis was born. I was thirty-two."

From the very beginning, Carl took an active role in Dennis's life. He wanted to help him learn how to learn by making it fun. He thought Dennis should play as much as possible, and have a good time. For more than ten years, they had a terrific time, sailing on the lakes, going to museums, doing all kinds of things. He took Dennis everywhere he went because when he had lived in that small town and had no kids, he had known a father who would come to the school, to social events, and even the local cafe with his little boy. Everywhere the father went, the kid was there, and people just got used to it. The two seemed to have a great relationship, so Carl figured that it was a good idea to take his child with him when he went to his adult activities. "I did that with my son," he says, "and he had a very good childhood. I'm sure of it. I'm sure that he will eventually realize that I was a very good father."

During all this, Donna stayed in the background, outside the intense activities Carl shared with Dennis. She played the traditional mother, teaching Dennis good habits like eating properly and brushing his teeth. Carl's career was taking off, too. His studies complete, he got a job teaching psychology at another university, published steadily, and achieved tenure.

He was forty-four when he began having an affair with one of his graduate students, and it destroyed both his marriage and his relationship with his son. "Dennis was so angry with me, so angry," Carl recounts. "He was thirteen, and I had betrayed him." After the divorce, Dennis maintained his distance even when he and his father were together—the distance of a teenager seeking independence distorted by the havoc Carl and his newfound love had wrought in Dennis's life. Then something terrible happened. Carl's girlfriend and her sister were killed in an auto accident on a snow-swept road in Colorado. At the time, Carl was with Dennis in Florida.

"When I heard that she had been killed, it crushed me," Carl says. "I sat by the phone for a long time and just couldn't believe it. Dennis was with me there in the hotel, and I told him. His reaction was . . . well . . . happy. He was happy that she had died. He was only fourteen. I realized that, but when he reacted that way, I was so hurt. It hurt me that my own son could totally ignore my grief, my feelings about this woman. Even if what I had done had angered him, I could not believe he would want revenge. I drew away from him at that moment. We became closer years later, but there in Florida, he drew blood."

The next five years were, in Carl's words, "a descent into my inner self." He felt guilty about his divorce, his son, and the young woman who had died. He was astonished that his relationship with her had been marked by so much destruction.

Carl came out of his daze at fifty when he met Cathy. She was forty-one years old, a mother of two teenage girls, and a schoolteacher like Donna. Although Cathy was reluctant, Carl wanted a child. She was mainly concerned about her age—she was forty-four when Kevin was born—but it was a perfect pregnancy and birth. She even got her master's degree the same year.

"It's different this time because I'm different," Carl explains. "I still try to make him believe in himself the way I did with Dennis, and to be able to learn and adapt to changes. But I am less goal-oriented because I have learned how many things that you have no control over can intervene in your life. I don't necessarily spend more time with Kevin, either. I've always been against these quantity measures of time, anyway. It's the quality. A lot of men count being at home with their children as sleeping on the sofa while the kids watch TV."

Did Carl want to have this child to soothe his guilt about the divorce and what had happened with Dennis? He does not think so. He looks at it more as trying to recover through fathering, something he always loved in himself and then missed. "It's very selfish and egotistical, in a way," he says. "But the whole process is just so enjoyable. It's a way to enjoy life. So why not enjoy it in our fifties if that's what we like? It's the most meaningful thing I do. And because I am fulfilling myself, I am much better for everyone around me, including my first son, who accepts this marriage and my new child. This is what life is about, really. I'm happy—that's the bottom line for me."

Other versions of recovery are more obviously laced with a heavy dose of post-divorce guilt about earlier father-child relationships. Like John (above), Frank is also sixty-five and retired. But unlike John, Frank looks back on his fathering at an earlier age with a dark dissatisfaction that explains almost everything about his role as a parent so late in life. It's not easy for him to tell us about his relationship with his older children—four boys, now twenty-nine to forty years old. He needs to lead us to it through his odyssey, beginning with his divorce in 1969.

"I was forty when I got divorced," he says. "The kids ranged from four to fifteen. It was tough. I lived alone for a while, and then I had an intervening marriage which lasted for five years. During that marriage I got a vasectomy. She did not have her own kids, and I did not want any more children. I mean, I had had enough. I'd been through that stuff and wasn't interested in pursuing it again. I don't know if this is too hard on me or not, but that marriage was one of convenience, in the sense that we cohabitated and were very happy together, but at least I always sort of knew that it was not going to be permanent. The point was, I needed help. Even though two of my sons came to live with me, I needed psychic and physical support, and they couldn't give it to me. She was a part-time schoolteacher and artist and I was working full-time. So we got a house, and one kid lived with us until he got married himself, and the other one, who was about fourteen then, was at a private school a few hours away, and he would come on vacations. As I said, it was a marriage of convenience. The getting together, our life together, and the parting were not traumatic. So, after five years I was alone again."

He met Sandy, his current wife, a year later. She was working as a nurse at a hospital in Boston. "We talked over our relationship a lot," he says. "She must have cried a dozen times. She's twenty-one years younger than I am. The discussions produced a lot of anxiety for me, but my life was changing and we got married four years later.

"We had discussed children when we first met. I mean, she was only twenty-nine, and if she was going to enter into a relationship she was going to think about kids. But I never let it in. I was not willing to consider it, and so she didn't press it. But it bubbled back up after my mother's death. She died in the fall, and the following spring I contracted cancer—a form of Hodgkin's disease. It was all very traumatic for us. And after that, after my mother's death and my bout with cancer, all of a sudden casting a shadow beyond one's death became very important.

"I did a lot of reading then. I had become aware of theorists who feel that genetic heritage is codeterminant with cultural heritage. What one can do to influence a child is not a great deal, unlike the genetic stuff that you pass on to kids. You can destroy or build a life with either—either the genetic or cultural stuff. Once I believed that, my vasectomy and my own genes became less relevant to me. It got to be a horse I could ride, if I can use that metaphor. Suddenly, having a child in order for Sandy to be monogamous with me was just something that would preserve our relationship and would live on beyond me, for us together. It became doubly important for me because this marriage was erasing the pain of my first marriage. This one was the one I wanted to leave my imprint on.

"The children from the first marriage represented something so different to me, sad as I am to say that. My boys and I enjoyed a good relationship, you know, in a family. But my first wife and I were quite at odds with each other. When we finally broke up, it was not a very pleasant breaking. And although the boys and I still maintain a very close relationship—as a matter of fact, my oldest boy and I were partners in business for a while—I felt as though there were a lot of things that I had done in that first go around that I would like to make better. If I had a chance to do it again, I figured, I could really knock the socks off this thing.

"My fourth child was born while I was in school in Boston. I would have prevented it if I could. I knew that my relationship was coming apart and I had developed a pretty severe rage in my life. She was sleeping around, and although I did not know this at first, when I finally became aware of it, I did a real job on myself.

"She would never punish the children. She would ask me to do it. I'd get home from work, and she would regale me with the sins of the day we were in. I began to be the punisher. And it was so exasperating because she wasn't happy to handle it, and I couldn't either when I was away all the time. So I struck them. I would use my hand at first, but then I began to use a belt to strap them. I hurt them. I don't think I ever drew blood, but I sure laid some welts. And as things began to come apart, I got a job in another state, and I took the family with me under my wife's protest. We got there, and the oldest boy got into drugs. I sort of intensified the punishment aspect. One day, I was acting in an amateur play and the part in the play involved losing my temper — getting angry — and I learned what it was like to really lose my temper. And it came to me that in my rage at the children, I was really striking their mother, I mean, it helped me figure things out. I took the kids out one night in the car, and I sat them up on the fender of the car, and stared them up and down and I said, now look, let me tell you what's been happening. I've got to tell you I've been very angry at your mother and I've beat you and it's not fair to you, and I will never spank you again. And I have not. I have never struck any of the children again.

"But I feel very bad about it nevertheless. The kids and I have talked about it over the years so that I think we've come to terms over it. After the divorce, I got to be very close with them, and they've stayed close to each other, too. There's still a void, though. A guilt. And having learned this about myself, I felt that I could have a relationship with a new child that would be, you know, much, much better. The cancer tipped it over, but it was this need, this deep need to do it once more, this time with no anger and no pain.

"I told Sandy, let's do it, and we did. We got donated sperm, and I have never been sorry. I have this wonderful little girl, and I have very intense feelings about her. When I was young I was a workaholic, on the road fifty to sixty percent of the time. Now, I'm retired, have a lot of time, and spend it all with my daughter. We do a lot of craft things together. I'm pretty good with my hands. We do calligraphy, and we have adventures. We go out into the marshlands and look at the pickle weed and the goose flocks, and the wild flowers. We bring them in and try growing them. We collect things. At the crack of dawn we take off and go to the lighthouse down at the coast and spend the night there and get up early to walk on the beach. I mean, this is stuff that I would have loved to have done with my boys, and did do when they were older. It's all been a big awakening, and now I am getting a chance to do it right."

Although John, Carl, and Frank's stories are unique, they are also typical of stories that most refathers tell. Because younger fathers are so involved in their work, and have a fifty-fifty chance of getting divorced (most after only seven or eight years of marriage), divorce and the sense of incompleteness about fatherhood is as much the norm for fathering in America as is the idealized version of the full-term father in the stable, two-parent family. Recovering fatherhood, as these men are doing, could become more prevalent, depending on the choices that men in late middle age make. Second-chance children, raised in close, intense relations with nurturing dads, could be a counterpoint to a much larger group of children of divorce, emotionally distant from or even hostile to their fathers.

OLDER FIRST-TIME FATHERS

Not all older fathers we interviewed had had children before. Some had never even wanted them. These cases are quite rare in the post–World War II generation because of the great emphasis put on marriage and family. Even men who, deep in their hearts, did not especially want families, felt socially compelled to marry and father. The economics of marriage and family also favored such behavior in the 1950s and 1960s. Jobs were plentiful and purchasing power rose steadily. Men now in their fifties could think about having kids when they were in their mid twenties because the world was their oyster. They could think about buying a home for twenty or thirty thousand dollars at twenty-seven years of age because they could easily save the down payment in three or four years. They got a job, worked their way up the ladder, consumed more each year, and had a great future. Why *not* marry and have kids?

The men who did not buy into this scheme were "outsiders." If they weren't suspected of being homosexual, they were at best regarded as socially strange, "terminally single" men whose characters were flawed by some deep psychological problems — a source of endless party conversations for amateur Freudians. They were holdouts in the mass rush to embrace the American dream.

Finding such men today in their post-midlife bouncing a baby begs for an explanation. Is the same eccentric contrariness that made them choose bachelorhood in the heyday of families also pushing them into this unconventional choice? As they reached this "certain age," did they perhaps find a certain emptiness in their lives, an emptiness accentuated by the specter of old age? What kind of father does thirty years of family abstinence produce?

What we found should not surprise. Some older men, once they found the time and the right women to marry, were eager to have a child. Others entered family life reluctantly, even when happy in a relationship. Yet once fathers, even the reluctant men were enthusiastic, involved, and often surprised at their own reaction. These older fathers have all the nurturing, calmer qualities of middle-aged men, with their better understanding of time and what remains behind, and do not carry any of the positive or negative baggage of earlier fatherhood.

We met Colin at the wedding of a friend. Now in his mid fifties, Colin had been so wrapped up with becoming a doctor and then practicing surgery when he was younger that he did not have time for marriage. "At first, my mother thought I wasn't trying hard enough to meet someone," he says, chuckling. "But when I turned forty and still hadn't hooked up with anyone, she started asking indirect questions about my sexuality. She was sure I was gay and was leading a seamy, underground life that no one knew about. I could tell that it was driving her crazy—her only son a gay doctor. It was almost too much. The more I tried to reassure her, the worse it was."

When Colin was forty-five and his mother had just about given up hope, he met a Dutch anesthesiologist who was spending her sabbatical at the hospital where he worked. She was almost forty herself, had never been married, and also had a mother who worried about her. "We were birds of a feather," Colin says. "We could joke about our work, our age, and our mothers. Even though we were brought up on different sides of the ocean, we had had amazingly similar experiences." They didn't have to think twice about getting married.

Both wanted a child. "Then the real miracle happened," Colin says, speaking louder over the wedding reception band. "Sean was born. It was the greatest thing that could have happened to me, and made me wonder why I had waited so long to have kids. I scaled down my practice and turned more to teaching, which let me spend more time at home. Birgit got certified here in the U.S., but only worked part-time. So we took parenting seriously and enjoyed it. We still liked our work—I get a real kick teaching the next generation of surgeons—but we had already proved to ourselves that we were good at what we did and were making enough money that we did not have to kill ourselves just to make more. Family life gave us the balance we didn't have when we were younger."

Once Colin reached a certain age and met someone with whom he felt comfortable, he had no doubt that he wanted to marry and have a child. He was an old bachelor but not a committed one.

But some bachelors have no desire to have a family. Rick, "the philosopher," as he was known to many of his friends, was always envied by his married friends for his commitment-free life. He was a freelance consultant, which made it seem that he was not quite as successful professionally as they were, but he always had a lot more money for himself and a much better time. His friends' wives distrusted him for what he represented and for his polygamous behavior.

"I didn't want to have a family just to have one," he says. "It would have been dishonest. That's why I didn't do it at twenty-five when all my friends were getting married, or thirty-five when my family and friends were pressuring me beyond belief, or at forty-five when I had the money and lots of women who would have been happy to share it with me. It just was not in me to settle down. I was having a great time — lots of friends, travel, living abroad when I felt like it. I never figured I wanted a kid. I was leading a pretty full life without one, and all these people I know who have families would, one way or another, let me know that I was lucky. I had freedom, and was doing what I wanted to do. I didn't miss having a family at all."

Suddenly, though, Rick changed. At least, that's the way it seemed, but the process was actually much longer than that. He met Sylvia in his late forties and she became one of his "friends," as he called them. She was fifteen years younger than he, and she knew she was not alone in his affections but did not seem to mind. In fact, she appeared to be the only woman in town who did not want to get married, did not have kids, and did not want them. Although she was childless, she had been told she could not have children, so there was no pressure from her biological clock to get married.

As the years passed, Rick found himself relaxing more and more with her. Meanwhile, Sylvia was creeping further and further into his tent, organizing herself in his apartment, first when he was away on trips, then even when he was there.

"At some point, I fell in love with this woman," Rick notes, almost as if he is observing someone else's life. "I felt good with her, and stopped wanting to see anyone else. It took a long time for me to admit this to myself. First, I resisted by thinking that it was only okay for a few days at a time. Then, I thought that it was okay if I kept my own space. Even that argument fell by the wayside."

When Rick came back from one of his trips, Sylvia told him she was pregnant but that the doctors strongly doubted the pregnancy would last. She also made clear that she had her own doubts whether she should have a child, since she did not really want one. "She told people that the reason she chose me was that I did not want to have kids. She was very definite about that because she had had a few relationships that broke up because she could not have children.

"My attitude during the whole pregnancy was that, damn it, I wanted to live without it —I don't need it, I don't want it, it's going to complicate my life. Things with Sylvia are going so well. God knows what this is going to do. But then, at the fifth month, we realized that the baby was going to happen, and Sylvia said, 'let's see what happens,' so what could I do? I decided in my own mind to take things as they came. That's the way I am. I couldn't do anything about it. Life is life. Whatever happens, happens."

Rick's son was born in the middle of Rick's fifty-fifth year. He was to have been out of town for the birth, allowing him to preserve some distance from the event, but as fate would have it, the pregnancy went past the due date, and he was there to witness his son's birth. It transformed him almost immediately into a doting father—one whose conversation became almost instantly boring to his now older friends for its trite obsession with infant achievements.

"It was quite moving, really. I had seen Joshua in the new baby room—the nurse had held him up for me—but I was with Sylvia in the room when I really got to see him for the first time, to hold him. They brought him in before his first bath. The three of us in the room together . . . it left me with a feeling that I had never had before."

Rick's life changed. When he talks about it, he likes to make fun of himself, to allow his old friends to tease him about his former uncompromising attitude toward family life. "I don't have the impression that I'm different," he says. "I mean, objectively, you could probably say that I am, but, you know, I'm doing my thing. I've got a new element in my life which is a lot of fun. It's an incredible pleasure. I'm not even sure what it is that makes it pleasurable. Even sometimes the crying, believe it or not. Because then it becomes a challenge to get him to stop crying. I walk around with him and try to talk him out of it and heave him over my shoulder and try to dance with him. I find it all a pleasure, the crying, the playing with him when he is alert, and just looking at him. He's so cute. He looks like me. And you know all those dumb, ridiculous things that people say about having kids? It turns out that there is something to it. I hate to admit it, but it's true."

The other part of having a child that surprised Rick was the way it affected his relationship with Sylvia. He had always avoided commitment, so it was natural to believe that a child—the ultimate commitment—would trigger an adverse reaction to the person who had foisted this thing on him. But when Joshua arrived, the relationship deepened. Rick saw Sylvia in a different role, operating differently, managing differently, and he liked it. He liked the idea that he was in love with her and that they had a child together.

Rick could still claim "outsider" status—the eccentric difference that always separated him from others. He had all the pleasures of youth when others were struggling in families. Now he has tired of the running around and is ready to settle down to the pleasures of fathering. In a sense, Rick feels he has given up nothing. Maybe he will not see Joshua's children, but then again, he will have the childhood of his own son to enjoy. "I have turned life upside down," he says. "And why not?"

These late first-time fathers react with intensity to their new loves. They seem genuinely surprised by the pleasure they get from infants and toddlers, and play father roles with the patience and wisdom of older age. Even if their energy levels are lower, they have less need to use that energy for other activities.

Whether late fatherhood is a first-time experience or a repeat performance, today's middle-aged men seem much more likely to make fatherhood the centerpiece of their lives. We think that one reason it has had such a large impact on these men is that they have less time left in life, so their relationship with their children is that much more important to them. They also tend to have more time each day to spend with the children. And for some, emerging from unhappy experiences in the first round of fathering, it is a chance to recover their self-image as a decent human being capable of loving and raising a child. The patience and attention that characterize this more "grandfatherly" approach to fathering appears, more than anything, to be wonderfully encouraging to children and to have most of the features of what psychologist Jerrold Lee Shapiro defines very simply as "good fathering." In his words:

> The good father is available for his children. He is able to show them his interest, love, and caring. He teaches them values by words and actions. He understands their needs from a child's perspective, yet he maintains his protective parental role. The good father encourages his children to experiment within proper limits. He allows his children to know him well enough that they may incorporate him into their personal psychological selves. He shares with them his pride at their accomplishments and his own. He is always available in times of crisis.[3]

4

. . . .

Older Men and Younger Women

Kate, a twenty-nine-year-old mother of twins, is on a trip to Nova Scotia with her husband, John, when the housekeeper at the fishing lodge where they are staying asks her, "So, did your father catch anything today?" Kate glares at the housekeeper, then walks away, not bothering to tell her that John, who is fifty-two, is her husband.

Back home a few weeks later, a teenager, watching John play with the children, says, "Those kids really get along with their grandpa. That's pretty cool."

Then there are the looks—the daggers that women, and especially middle-aged women, shoot at her with their eyes. It does not happen often, but it happens. And although Kate says the looks don't really bother her anymore because she is used to them, she sometimes wishes people could see things through her eyes.

"So often, we're just looked upon as the 'younger woman' or 'the new, improved model' that the big bad ex-husband traded in for his ex-wife," she says. "And that seems to explain everything. But for me, the issue of why I married an older man and decided to have children with him isn't so simple."

Although most middle-aged fathers are married to women fewer than ten years their junior, there are still many older men pushing strollers with much younger wives walking by their side. Our society continues to regard such age-gap couples with a certain amount of disdain. The critics may not be loud or overtly judgmental, but you can hear them talking in the privacy of their own homes or whispering their theories in the background at parties and other public places.

"The nerve," a woman whispers to her friend, observing a fifty-five-year-old man with his thirty-three-year-old wife. "She could be his daughter."

"Has to be his money," the friend whispers back. "Why else would a young woman marry a man his age?"

To most people, it seems obvious why an older man would be in a relationship with a younger woman. She is young, and that is reason enough in our youth-oriented society, where we are bombarded with ads that tell us, *Be young, have fun, drink Pepsi*; *Life is short, play hard*; and, of course, *Just do it*. These messages are hard to ignore, and for the older man whose tummy is expanding and hairline receding, a young woman becomes his means of warding off old age and proving to his peers that he's still got "it."

There, are, of course, less superficial reasons why older men marry younger women. Many of the men we spoke to said that after years of being in a gradually deteriorating, senses-dulling relationship with a first wife, they found the spark they were looking for in a younger woman. "She has inspired me to do things I didn't think I was capable of doing," several men told us. And, "She opened up whole new avenues and vistas that I didn't realize existed."

While that sounds noble in a *carpe diem* sort of way, it still implies that her youth — and in this case, a more youthful perspective — is the driving force in a man's love for a younger woman. To the casual observer, this makes perfect sense. Youth is attractive. But when we try to explain why a younger woman, especially a woman in her twenties, marries an older man, it just does not make sense to say that his "maturity" is the driving force in her love for him. There must be something else.

For certain older men — especially those getting married for the first time — one major reason for marrying a younger woman is to have children. But most older men have already "been there and done that" — they have been married before and have children who are either grown up or on the verge of adulthood. The idea of starting from scratch and going through the rigors of child-rearing is not appealing. "This is a time when we should be enjoying life, doing things we've always wanted to do," they say to themselves. "The last thing we want is to saddle ourselves with another child, or children. We'll be stuck at home for the rest our lives."

For this larger group of older men, the question is how badly they want to be with a younger woman. "Maybe I can talk her out of having a baby," is a typical initial response. But the men who think that are deluding themselves. The stark reality is that children are as much the logical outcome of a July-December marriage as a July-July one.

The bright side of this conflict is the sweet contradiction that compromise can create. An older man falls in love with a younger woman and she falls for him. The relationship makes him feel youthful, handsome, charming. They marry and he agrees to have a child with her, which inevitably brings out the lurking soft side in him — the nurturing father — even more than it would in a younger man. In turn, this new attitude makes him more desirable to his bride, who thinks she has the perfect father for her children.

But, on the other hand, if a compromise is not reached at some point (preferably before marriage), the child issue can end up destroying a relationship. In the unhappiest of cases, a young woman married to an older man sees something in the relationship he has with his older children that discourages her from having children with him even if he would agree. This, too, is almost guaranteed to end their marriage.

OKAY, LET'S DO IT

The story of Deborah and Alex is representative of an older man–younger woman union. They met through a Jewish singles association in Buffalo, New York, and although it was not what Deborah described as "a match made in heaven," they got along well from the beginning and shared a lot of common interests. At first, Deborah did not think much about their age difference — when they met, Deborah was thirty-three, and Alex forty-eight — but focused instead on their similarities. They both came from similar religious backgrounds, and, just as important, they both had been divorced and seemed to know what they wanted from a second marriage.

The only difference was that Alex had three children and Deborah had none, which became a point of discussion when they began to contemplate marriage.

"I was very nervous when I told him I wanted to have children," she says. "Things had been going so well and I didn't want something to screw things up. And, of course, I knew he already had three children."

Initially, he put up some resistance, but in the end he told her he did not "mind" having a family with her. "He didn't endorse the idea one hundred percent," she says. "I'd say it was about seventy-five percent." But it still was a yes, and a few months later, they married. Today, they have a son, Adam, who is two.

We talked to Deborah about why she married an older man and some of the issues she faced starting a family with him.

"The first time I got married it was straight out of college to a guy I had been dating in college," she says. "At the time, we were both scared by the thought of going out into the real world, and we just thought it was the thing to do. I also think, on a certain level, that it was a way for both of us to get away from our families."

The "real world" turned out to be the rat race of New York City, and they quickly settled into it. Her husband was in finance, she was in advertising, and the stress of trying to keep their careers on track eventually began to take its toll on their relationship.

"When I got married to Alex, one of the benefits I saw in marrying him was that he had already done the whole career route and was in semiretirement. I didn't want to support someone emotionally in terms of a career again. That wasn't the lifestyle I wanted. Really, I wanted to relax. Be able to go on vacations. When my first husband and I were in our twenties we never did that and neither did our friends."

However, there was a drawback to marrying a man who had the time and money to go on vacations. His children from his first marriage thought Deborah had only married him for his money. "There was initially some friction with his children from his first marriage," she says, "especially with the youngest girl, Sarah, who is now seventeen. She took his getting remarried the hardest and ended up saying some nasty things to him about me. In a way, I expected it, but it still hurt."

Deborah is only six years older than Alex's eldest child, Dean, but her age did not bother her husband's older children as much as the fact that he was getting remarried. "I know his ex-wife did not like that he was marrying a younger woman," she explains. "And she would say things to Sarah, who was still living at home with her, which would just fuel the fire. But I think that his kids would have been upset with whomever he married. I was in a no-win situation there. But I knew that going in and I accepted it."

What she did not know was that Alex was less financially secure than he had led her to believe, and last year, after almost four years of marriage and when their son Adam was only two years old, Deborah was forced to start working again. She became the primary breadwinner in the family. The unexpected upside was that her relationship with his older children improved. "His children thought he was really loaded. And that simply wasn't the case. Although I knew that from the beginning, I didn't think I would be going back to work as soon I have."

On the whole, she sees their child benefiting from having an older father. But Deborah does have a few complaints. "As a father of three grown-up children, Alex had seen everything already, so he didn't get stressed out over situations like I do. That can be a good thing, but it sort of bothered me because he wasn't letting me be a first-time mother. I'd be freaking out about something and he'd be very calm — like, don't worry about it, the child will be fine. In a way, I wanted him to be a little more nervous because I felt foolish being the stressed one."

Another conflict they have is over their vision of family. Although Alex agreed to have a child with Deborah, he then decided he did not want to have any more children.

"To him, one child is enough, because he already has three other children. That makes four in total, which seems to him very much like a family. But my concept of our family is just the three of us. And I'd like it to be more than that."

As Deborah is well aware, an older husband's children from a previous marriage can be a source of conflict in a marriage. But at the same time, they can also tell a woman a lot about what kind of a father her husband would make for her children. Several women we interviewed said they actually became more attracted to the idea of having children with the man they were dating (or were already married to) because he had a good relationship with his children.

For example, thirty-year-old Diana, from Los Angeles, recently married her former psychiatrist, Don, who is forty-eight years old and has a nine-year-old son, Ryan. Although Ryan doesn't live with his father, he is a frequent visitor to Don and Diana's home, and Diana has a close relationship with him. "We play a lot of sports together and he really likes that," she says. "He tells his friends how his dad married this woman who doesn't throw like a girl and they just think that's the coolest."

Although they have not had children yet, they are planning to, and Diana says she was partially drawn to Don because of his fathering skills and the fact that he and his ex-wife were cordial with one another. "I think all those things helped establish in my mind that he was a considerate, stable person. He and his ex-wife had made a mistake but they were making the best of it. I respected him for that. I also respected her."

Thirty-six-year-old Marilyn, from Ridgewood, New Jersey, also saw her husband-to-be as a responsible person because of the way he treated his children. But after being married for seven years, and having children of her own with him, she sometimes feels that she may have taken on more responsibility than she can handle.

"Seeing how he treated his children from his first marriage definitely had an influence on my decision to marry James," she says. "It made me see him as a responsible person and that was something that really appealed to me. I think, to a certain degree, when you want to be with someone, you just assume that he was the 'good guy' in the relationship with his ex-wife, and that she was the one who had the problem. That's probably a stupid way of looking at things, because it just isn't true, but at least when you see that he has a good relationship with his children — that he actually makes an effort to be with them and support them financially — you know that he didn't cop out, and that's reassuring."

Marilyn married a man eleven years older than she, who had two children — a ten-year-old boy and an eleven-year-old girl — from a previous marriage. Her case is unusual because James had joint custody of his children when Marilyn met him, and after they married, they sued and won full custody of the children.

"Convincing him to have more children wasn't a problem," Marilyn says. "He came from a big family and wanted more children. So that was the plan from the beginning."

What she did not plan for was the difficulty of trying to raise two young children of her own, as well as two teenagers. "I've always gotten along pretty well with James's children," she says. "I've lived with them since they were ten and eleven, which is a good age for children. But now that they are sixteen and seventeen, they're going through those moody, rebellious years, which is tough enough to deal with in itself. But I also have a one-year-old and a four-year-old who demand my constant attention. Their problems are much different than a teenager's problems. So it's quite a contrast and sometimes this place is a real madhouse."

Another thing she did not anticipate was James's diminished role as a father. Although she said he is wonderful to the children when he is with them, after they got married and had more children, he began to work harder and longer hours. Part of that was out of financial necessity, as it takes a lot more money to raise four children than two, but it was also because now that Marilyn had become the primary caretaker of his children, he found more time to concentrate on his career.

"Our situation is unusual in the sense that his first wife really didn't care about the children. She was off doing her own thing. So when I came along and was a 'good' mother, James saw that as an opportunity for him to focus on his career."

However, she did not entirely blame him for the situation. Before she had children, she had a career as a real estate broker, but she gradually gave that up as she discovered how rewarding motherhood could be. "I didn't realize how much I would enjoy being a mother," she says. "It took me by surprise. And I just decided that's what I wanted to do. That's how I wanted to spend my days."

So does she regret marrying a man who already had children?

"No, I don't regret it," she says. "But I wouldn't necessarily recommend it to a friend."

Jeanine is forty-four, but it was at least twelve years ago when she met her husband, Paul. They worked in the same department at an insurance company and sometimes would collaborate on accounts. He remembers the situation well. "We worked together, had similar professions, and, from my point of view, the personal relationship grew," he says. "I was married, so the issue was what to do. Ultimately I decided to get a divorce, and Jeanine and I got married." That was eight years ago. Paul was sixty and Jeanine thirty-six. Paul had three children from his first marriage, all in their mid to late twenties at the time.

Both knew full well before they married that Jeanine wanted to have her own child. "Well, she wanted to, I didn't," Paul explains. "I had to get to the point where I was willing to do it. But I understood that since Jeanine wanted a child and did not have children from a previous marriage, if we were going to get married, I was essentially obligated to agree. So getting married meant that we would have a child. I knew that the decision was one and the same. I just had to decide whether I was willing to give up a lot of things that I wanted to do in the late stages of my life for spending it with Jeanine. Because I also knew that having a young child was going to deny me the time to do a lot of those other things, especially realizing some of the business plans I had.

"So I went through the arguments lots of different ways in my head. I went through the altruistic argument—I should do it because I'm a good guy—and the argument that the relationship wouldn't be tranquil if I didn't agree. The one that convinced me, though, is that I really wanted to be with this young woman and that if I wanted to commit myself to her, this was the right thing to do."

For Jeanine, any other decision would have kept her from marrying Paul, even if he had already divorced his wife and even if she liked the way he related to his older children. She was happy that he came to the conclusion he did, but could not quite understand why he had such a hard time reaching it. "I just don't understand why, at sixty, he put such a high priority on his work," she says. "To me, having a child is so much more important than trying to reach these idealized goals that men set up. Then they blame the fact that they did not achieve their ambitions or that they could not do this or that because they had a family. There are usually a lot of other reasons, and so what, anyway. But I have to say this about Paul," she admits, smiling. "Despite my complaints about his priorities, he turned out to be a dedicated father. That made me feel stronger about our relationship, and watching him with little Chris somehow made Paul seem younger, not older."

The age gap may have seemed smaller for Jeanine when she watched Paul play with their five-year-old, but the generational difference between them produced frequent disagreement on child-rearing. Paul had been very influenced as a first-time father by the 1960s philosophy of giving children a lot of freedom to define their own limits, while Jeanine, who grew up in the 1960s, thought that limits were really needed. "I see Paul letting Sean do just about anything he wants," she says. "The interesting thing is that Paul's older kids think that he didn't put enough limits on them. I thought it was because he was working so hard when they were growing up, so he wasn't really around. But now I can see that he just doesn't like telling Sean what to do and not do. I can't stand it—I end up being the enforcer around here."

We found that child-rearing styles are a matter of disagreement in other July-December relationships as well, especially because much older dads usually have a lot more time to get involved with raising their young children. The teenage daughter of one couple we interviewed reported that the thirty-year age difference between her forty-year-old mother and seventy-year-old father was most apparent when it came to dealing with the daughter's behavior. "My father is much more conservative when it comes to my comings and goings and who my friends are," she explains. "I guess he has values about those things from the 1950s, or something like that. When it comes to my schoolwork, though, he thinks that the way they are teaching us in school is much too rigid—he wants more freedom in the way we learn. He keeps saying you can learn from everything, not just from schoolwork. My mom is just the opposite. She is willing to give me more freedom to choose my friends and hang around with boys, but is a lot stricter about schoolwork. They don't exactly fight about it, but I can tell that my mom and he are miles apart."

SOME DON'T GIVE IN

So far, we have told stories that describe older men—whether they were resistant at first or not—as willing to compromise with their younger wives and have children. But some older men are truly reluctant to have children. This is what Charlotte confronted in her relationship with Jim.

"The last thing I had on my mind when I met Jim was marrying a guy his age," Charlotte, thirty-two, tells us. "I was twenty-five and he was forty-three. But I just got swept away. On our third date, we went to Spain. Whoever heard of going to Spain on a third date?"

When they met, Charlotte was working as an analyst for an investment bank on Wall Street and Jim had just started his own business after a career as a management consultant. It was by all accounts a whirlwind romance: New York's best restaurants, theater, opera, and long walks in Central Park, not to mention the trip to Spain. At first, she was shocked by the intensity of his courtship. By their second date, he was already talking about marriage and making promises she did not think he would keep. "I just kind of smiled a lot and thought, this guy must want to sleep with me really badly," she says.

But when they finally did sleep together and his talk of marriage continued, she began to realize he was sincere. With that realization, she began to drop her guard, and slowly found herself becoming more and more seduced by the lifestyle he offered her. Did she love him? "I don't think I did," she admits. "But at that age, twenty-four, I was a lot more vulnerable than I am now. He gave me a lot of attention. He called me all the time. He always wanted to know how I felt about things. And I really liked that."

He was also good-looking, charming, had a lot of money, and was starting an exciting new business. Charlotte reckons that he was looking for a certain type of woman — someone who was a certain age and who had a certain look — and that she happened to be at the right place at the right time, or, depending on how you look at it, the wrong place at the wrong time. "He was definitely looking for a younger woman," she says. "He's admitted that to me. But he said that was only a small part of why he was taken by me."

Still, after they were married, there were a great many times when she was made to feel like a "trophy." Her husband told her how to dress and act. He tried turn her into his conception of what his wife should be, which made her feel objectified. Also, the people they socialized with were generally older — in their late thirties and forties — and Charlotte stood out. At first, she just felt privileged to be there and to be accepted by his friends. But then she began to miss some of the freedom her friends had. While they envied her, she was envious of them. "I couldn't really hang out with them, though," she says. "I mean, my husband didn't want me in bars and places like that."

The other big change she experienced when she got married was that she stopped working on Wall Street and began to take acting lessons. In that sense, having a husband to support her was a great advantage because it allowed her to do what she really wanted. And Jim did not mind that she had stopped working because he wanted her home as much as possible.

Surprisingly, however, as she began to become unsatisfied with the marriage, it was not Jim who suggested they have children, but Charlotte. From the outset Jim had told her he did not want children. "We talked about it just before we were going to get married, and he said he really didn't want children. By then, I had already agreed to get married and was set to go through with it, so I wasn't going to back out just because he said he didn't want children. And besides, I didn't really believe him. I mean, I just thought when push came to shove he would want them. After all, he didn't have any, and it just seemed absurd that he wouldn't change his mind at some point."

But why did she want children if she felt the marriage was on shaky ground?

"Well, part of me just thought it was time. At that point, I was twenty-nine and my biological clock was ticking. I always wanted children and here I was married, why shouldn't I have children?"

But she admits that the other half of her desire may have had to do with the fact that he was saying no. She began to question his love for her. "It got to the point where I was like, is this all I am to you, someone you can show off to your friends? If you love me — if you really love me — you'll give me a child. It got to be that sort of a game."

After saying no for several months, Jim finally relented and agreed to try to have a child. But there was a catch. He put a three-month time limit on how long they could try.

"It was like a business deal," she says. "I had this option to procreate and if I didn't exercise it then, that was going to be it. That was my shot."

She took it, but felt tremendous pressure, because by that time she was not even sure anymore if she wanted to have a child. He felt he had compromised, but in reality, it only made her feel worse.

Ultimately, she did not conceive a child in the time allotted, but today she sees her failure to conceive as a blessing. At thirty-two, she is divorced, and trying to make up for what she calls her "lost twenties." But she adds that her view of being married to an older man is not entirely negative.

"Being single now in my early thirties, I'm finding that men my age really aren't ready to settle down. I know that's a gross generalization, but it just seems as if a lot of men feel they have to achieve certain goals before they commit themselves to a woman. They have this idea that once they reach a certain point they will be suddenly ready to settle down. Sometimes those goals are reasonable and attainable. But too often now, with the economy the way it is, and things in general just being more competitive for men, they really aren't. So women in their early thirties are finding themselves going out with older men because they are the ones that are ready — either because they achieved the goals they set for themselves or they simply came back down to earth. So my feeling is I'll probably end up with an older man. The difference will be that this time I'll be ready."

"I DON'T KNOW
WHAT THE FUTURE HOLDS FOR US"

"I don't really think about what our relationship will be like ten years from now," says Beth, a twenty-seven-year-old married to a man thirty years her senior. The statement betrays the disappointing lessons Beth has already learned about her husband, Tom, as a potential father. It is not that Tom does not want to have any more children, but that Beth is not sure whether she would like him to father *her* children. This has kept her focused on enjoying "the here and now."

"I didn't tell my parents for a while how old he was," she says. "They knew he was older because they met him. And my mother kept asking how old he was and I kept saying, it doesn't matter. Finally, after we were married, I told them. They were shocked, but they've accepted it. My father is actually five years younger than Tom, and they get along great. I mean, it's scary how well Tom and my father get along."

The way she talks, it sounds as though Beth is the mature one in the relationship, and when you look at her, she appears much older than her years. Whether she was born mature we do not know, but when she describes some of the responsibilities she has had to face marrying Tom, we begin to understand how she might have grown up in a hurry.

Tom has three children from two previous marriages. From his first wife, he has a girl, Jessica, who is now thirty-one and married. And from his second wife, two boys, Scott and Sean. When she was eighteen, Jessica was diagnosed schizophrenic, and was in and out of a mental institution for two years; Sean, the older of the two boys, was in a car accident when he was twenty and has been blind ever since; and Scott, the youngest, now twenty-one, is currently in a drug rehab center.

We wonder why a young, attractive woman would want to get locked into a relationship with a man who was not only thirty years her senior but who was carrying all this baggage. Was it money? No, she says. "His children think he's swimming in money. But the truth is he isn't. We're comfortable now, but we really need to make some good investments or we're going to be in trouble ten years from now." She pauses a moment, then says: "I guess I do think of our future in those terms."

Meanwhile, she does not feel his children are as big a burden as one might expect. "First of all," she says, "anybody you marry is going to have baggage. And these kids are at an age where they're becoming less dependent on their father. That's how I looked at it."

However, Tom's children and his handling of them have had an effect on her image of him as a father. "He's a very giving father," she says. "But he gives in the wrong ways, and that bothers me. He only knows how to give money."

Tom does not want more children and, for the moment, Beth does not want them either. However, she is fairly certain that if she really wanted children, he would agree. "But the truth is," she says, lowering her voice, "and you can't tell him this — but if I wanted children, I wouldn't want to have them with him. I love him dearly, but he's not the father I would want for my children. But who knows, interview me in ten years and I might have something very different to tell you. I don't know what the future holds in store for us. I wish I did, but I don't. All I know about is right now. And right now, he's the man for me."

IS THE AGE GAP ALL THAT BAD?

In January 1993 an article appeared in the English newspaper, the *Daily Mail,* under the headline, "Is the Sexy Image of the Older Man Simply a Modern Myth?" The article went on to describe the findings of Maggie Jones, a journalist who wrote a book called *Marrying an Older Man.*

"The fact is, you're quite likely to end up divorced whatever age you marry," Jones told an interviewer, "but if someone has made you happy for a long time you're probably quite willing to look after them. Looking after an older partner only becomes a burden if you don't love that person."

For her book, Jones, married eleven years to a man eighteen years her senior, interviewed several dozen younger wives. She heard her share of negative comments, especially when the conversation turned to the topic of sex. Many younger wives, the book pointed out, secretly (and with good reason) fear that their husbands will lose their sexual appetites in their sixties and seventies as they themselves remain sexually active. Burying such fears was bound to cause problems for the couple, Jones said.

But far more important was discussing the child issue before marriage and coming to a mutually acceptable decision before it became "a deepening source of pain and conflict."

Of the younger women we interviewed, the ones that seemed most likely to stay in their marriages to older men were those who had defined clearly and realistically for themselves and their husbands what they expected in terms of having children. Deborah, Diane, Marilyn, and Jeanine are cases in point. For all the difficulties they face in their marriages, they had been straightforward about their desire to have children and to find in their husbands the good, caring fathers they expected. For all but Marilyn, these older men fit the pattern of having a lot more time to spend with their children.

Women are much more likely to be clear about these priorities when they marry later rather than earlier. But we were surprised to find that in many age-gap marriages, even when women in their late twenties and thirties marry older men, both partners fail to take a hard look at the future and plan accordingly. Some of the women we talked to had married without coming to terms with the possibility that their roles might have to be redefined in the future. In fact, to a large degree, they had succeeded in downplaying (or even ignoring) both future parenting and age issues in their relationships with their husbands. Time and time again, we heard women in their early thirties describing their fiftysomething husbands as "young at heart" or commenting, "he just doesn't act old so I don't think of him as old," but avoiding the possibility that this youthful demeanor might not extend to fathering.

That said, one of the more favorable aspects of a relationship with an older man who already has children, according to the women we interviewed, is that "you get a good picture of the kind of father he would be for your own children." Beth got an unfavorable picture of Tom as a father and will probably leave the marriage if she wants to have children, but most other women we talked to married their older husbands in part because they liked what they saw in them as fathers.

There are other advantages. To give a fair view of the pros and cons of much younger women being married to older men, we should compare that situation to a more usual real-life alternative: young women getting involved with men approximately their own age. The main reason that younger women are attracted to older men is because of the greater stability and higher incomes these men offer. Raising children in a better economic environment is not just a short-term advantage. If the marriage should be cut short either by divorce or her husband's death, wife and children have a pretty good chance to remain reasonably well-off. As we have seen, that is not always the case. But on average, the divorced wife or widow of an older man can count on at least some financial help.

The same is much less true for the divorced wife of a younger man. The ex-wife of a younger man and her children are likely to end up with a low income—mainly what she can earn from her own work. And she is more likely to get divorced within a few years of getting married than a woman the same age who marries a much older man. Even an older husband's death is a much less likely event than divorce in a young marriage.

If women got married believing that the marriage would only last seven to ten years, they might well do better marrying a man twenty years older. Of course, that is not the way most people enter into marriage. They meet someone they like and feel comfortable with and believe their relationship will last forever. If there is a large difference in age, they are more likely to question the consequences of their feelings, but even then, it seems that emotions push longer-term considerations way down the list. Despite all the bad things that can be said about older men–younger women marriages, we could be just as negative about the consequences of marriages between men and women in their twenties. Yet those marriages are considered normal, so what happens to them and to the children that come from them — no matter how sad and harmful — is also viewed as normal.

5

· · · · · · · · · · · · · · ·

The Adoption Connection

Typically, men who marry or remarry in their forties and fifties do so with women who are more than thirty-five years old and in the twilight of their child-bearing years. For these couples, trying to conceive a child is often a frustrating and difficult experience, made even more complicated by advances in fertility-enhancing techniques. In today's world, when a woman's biological clock is on its last ticks or her husband's sperm is deemed weak or impaired, there is always one more option to pursue, and one more medical expert to consult. This quest for parenthood can take a couple on a journey through fertility-enhancing drugs, sperm donations, and, if they can spare the thousands of dollars for each attempt, in-vitro fetal implants. Ask those who have made this journey about their experiences and you will always get a story, though it is usually filled with disappointment rather than elation.

"You put your money down, and you roll the dice," one man, Jim, tells us, after his wife's second in-vitro fetal implant didn't take. "You know the odds, but you try anyway. You're willing to try anything when you want something bad enough."

Stories like this are the folklore of a new culture—a culture shaped by women's professionalism, delayed marriage, and men remarrying in middle age. Most people, however, cannot afford to try expensive techniques. Enhancing fertility is usually not covered by health insurance, so by the time couples confront the prospects of in-vitro, the procedure's astronomical price and its high failure rate convince many that the adoption route to parenting makes a lot more sense.

We in the United States are lucky in this regard. Today, there are many roads to adoption, and they are all much smoother than in the past, especially if you get good advice to start with. Talk to couples in Europe and you find that state agencies still monopolize the process, and very low fertility rates make few children available—and the ones who are available are rationed out to younger people. There are also long waiting periods—several years in most cases. So most Europeans take their search abroad, to low-income countries, where they compete with Americans in what has become a big and sometimes shadowy business.

For older couples, adoption in the U.S. used to be difficult, if not impossible, too. A generation ago, the only adoption method was the traditional system of "closed" adoption, in which agencies controlled the adoption process and limited their applicants to parents who fit "normal" parenting criteria, meaning that both parents had to be under thirty-five to forty years old and usually had to be of the same race (and sometimes the same religion) as the child who was put up for adoption.[1]

Under the closed system, adoptive parents and the adopted child never knew the identity of the birth parents, and birth parents only knew the agency to whom they had given their child. Once children were cleared for adoption by the state's regulating bodies, the agencies received them from their birth mothers, then offered them to waiting adoptive parents from their prescreened lists. So it was the agencies, not the birth parents, that decided that middle-aged couples were unsuitable parents for young children.[2]

Not too long ago, this started to change. "Closed" adoption still predominates, still favors younger over older couples, and many states still require that couples work through agencies. But thanks to states such as California, many agencies are doing more "open" adoption. Adoption lawyers and counselors often work hand in hand with agencies to find children for parents seeking to adopt.[3] These professional matchmakers appeal directly to birth mothers who want to give up their babies. And now even agencies in closed adoption states are willing to assist in open adoptions for older parents, although these same agencies may favor younger parents for a closed adoption. With open adoption, individual choice reigns, allowing "extreme" groups, such as late-middle-aged couples, to play the game.

Lynne Fingerman, a leading adoption counselor who codirects the Adoption Connection, an agency that is part of Jewish Family and

Children's Services in San Francisco, told us, "In the ten years I have been doing this, the average age of adoptive parents has risen steadily, so that now the typical couple is in their late thirties, early forties. It's mainly the changing demographics and women postponing childbearing. So-called older couples don't look so old anymore."

Open adoption offers tremendous advantages, including shortening the waiting time for all couples, no matter what their age, because it expands the network of intermediaries bringing together potential adopters and adoptees; allowing birth mothers to interact directly with prospective adoptive parents and to choose between them; and giving prospective adopted parents an opportunity to learn about the birth mother and often the father, including their family health histories.

But at the same time, there are also obvious disadvantages to the open system, and if we focus on them here, it is because we don't want to glamorize an already difficult process.

HARD LESSONS

As we have explained, open adoption means that adoptive and birth parents interact during the pregnancy and possibly afterward. For various reasons, including economic need and state laws that prohibit transporting minors across a state line except by a legal guardian, a birth mother may even come to live with the prospective adoptive parents in the last month or so of pregnancy. This can make everyone feel very close, bonding adoptive parents to both mother and baby through a "shared pregnancy." But it can also be a difficult experience, turning into the worst of nightmares if the birth mother changes her mind about giving up the child.

For Ted and Sandra, that nightmare came true three years ago, when they were put in touch with a devout young Catholic who wanted to have her baby, then give him up for adoption. For her, it was a choice between keeping the baby or going to medical school. And for Ted and Sandra, it was initially a dream situation.

It was also one they never expected to be in. About six months after his younger son left home for college, Ted became seriously involved with a woman five years younger than he was. He did not think much about the consequences. He just knew that he was tired of awkward, pressurized dinner conversations with newly met women and of mornings after that were disastrous letdowns from the night before. It was not long before he met someone who seemed remarkably stable and resolutely solid — just the kind of nurturer who would make the perfect travel companion through middle age and beyond.

As important, Sandra was childless and did not want children. She had four brothers and sisters, taught dance to preschoolers, and had had enough of child care. Everything was just right: They fell in love, went jogging together, traveled to Europe, and had independent incomes and independent checking accounts. It was ideal.

But somehow, for some reason Ted can't entirely explain, a year later they were married and pregnant. When they met, they talked about them, not children. But love produces interesting desires. At thirty-nine, as the fertility door was closing, his solid companion through middle age began to see him as the man with whom she wanted to have a child. He could have said no, but he understood how important this issue had become to her and how important she had become to him. So, with great trepidation and fascination at his willingness to "return to his past," he gave in, and before he knew it, was on the road to becoming a late-middle-aged father.

The road was much longer than they expected. That first pregnancy did not work and neither did two others. In fact, the fertility door had already closed. They had become a couple searching for a child. Ted did not grasp it all then, but the failure to produce their own child and the ensuing adoption process began a transformation for him. He and Sandra had long, emotional talks about what it meant to lose three babies that they had seen on sonograms. Then, even as they were still trying next-to-last-ditch fertilization methods, a close friend and obstetrician put them in touch with the young woman who wanted to give up her baby.

"Here she was, a bright, beautiful woman who wanted to give us her baby," says Ted. "After all the disappointment we'd had over the past two years, it just seemed like a blessing."

They began attending adoption workshops, watched their birth mother get larger, and shared her increasingly complex feelings about her pregnancy. Listening to her, they sometimes felt uneasy, particularly when she told them about her angry feelings toward the child inside her, and her changing story about the father. But what they were hearing could not penetrate the massive wall of hope they had built around her and themselves.

In the adoption workshop, they were given warnings. "These relationships are complicated and often sour," they were told. But they did not believe it. Not ours, they thought.

Then the unthinkable happened: The birth mother, seven months pregnant, went to a lawyer in another city and got herself a set of adoptive parents whom she would never meet. Through their lawyer, Ted and Sandra learned that she had never felt comfortable with knowing her baby's adoptive parents and had used them as a "crutch" while she agonized over her dilemma and contemplated her choices. It had never occurred to them to bring in a professional counselor from day one to find out the birth mother's true feelings and to set up the rules of the relationship.

The lesson was a hard one, but Ted and Sandra were lucky. By attending an agency-sponsored adoption group, they were surrounded by other infertile parents and adoption experts who had ready advice for doing it right the next time.

"When our first attempt at adoption ended in disaster," Ted recalls, "that adoption group became our support group. The twenty of us around the room had heard adoption horror stories from successful adoptive parents who had been invited to speak to us and prepare us for the reality of disappointment along the way. But my wife and I were actually going through one of those horror stories as we were meeting. I blamed myself for the loss, believing that it was mainly my age that had made the birth mother reject us. But sharing those feelings with the group helped to heal the hurt and frustration. It also allowed us to come up with a better plan for the next round."

The first thing they did was prepare a photo-studded promotional brochure of themselves for their adoption lawyer to send out to prospective birth mothers. Preparing the brochure, they spent a lot of time wondering what it would be that would attract a young woman to a couple who was older than her parents.

"It was a little strange," Ted says. "It was like we were running for public office or something. We'd lost the first election, and now people were telling us this is how you run your campaign. You've got to be sophisticated yet honest."

But after their humbling experience with the first birth mother, they felt vulnerable. They need not have been concerned, though, Ted says, because it turned out that they matched many mothers' visions of what they wanted for their child. Their first birth mother hadn't found in them the couple she wanted, but others did.

He admits that he was surprised. Not just because of what happened to them the first time, but because he was influenced by what he calls our "ageist society."

"I had a hard time imagining that a woman the age of my older kids would pick me as a desirable parent for her child," he says. "But I was wrong. Even in an ageist society, we found that there are many who see other parenting criteria as more important than age, and some who saw middle age as a *plus* for lots of reasons."

Six months after sending their packet of brochures to their lawyer, Ted and Sandra found a baby girl. They first talked to their birth mother by phone when she was eight months pregnant, then met her two weeks later, and established an effortless yet profound relationship with her. Soon, they would find themselves standing in front of their adoption group, giving a speech similar to the ones they had heard months earlier, and offering the same advice as "successful" speakers before them.

"Be patient," they said. "Don't let your hope get the best of you. And never take anything for granted."

ROUGH BEGINNINGS, HAPPY ENDINGS

Eventually, all but one of the couples in Ted and Sandra's original group decided to adopt. And though their adoptions varied in complexity, they all ended up succeeding. The group had something else in common: They gave up on enhancing fertility early on. Most did hormone injections and sperm washings, but soon became convinced that adoption was the way to go.

In many ways, Ted and Sandra were lucky. Other couples we spoke to went through much more adversity and frustration, including the Michigan couple we're about to meet.

Sam and Sally are both doctors. You'd think that as doctors, they would have a comparative advantage in understanding their chances of overcoming barriers to conception. You would also expect that as professionals in the same field as gynecologists and obstetricians, doctors would have an easier time finding birth mothers and becoming knowledgeable about the adoption process.

But doctors run into the same problems as everyone else. The anecdotes they hear from local obstetricians about the hordes of birth mothers who want to give up their babies for adoption turn out to be exaggerated. And even when there is a birth mother available, doctors who try to handle the screening process without the help of a professional counselor end up courting disaster.

Sam is an internist. He has two older children from a previous marriage and did not want more, but when he divorced at forty-nine and married Sally two years later, everything changed. Sally was in her mid thirties, had been married before, and wanted, in Sam's words, "The closeness of a child, someone who would share her life, and, as she aged, would be able to have a relationship with her."

Unfortunately, Sam had had a vasectomy at thirty-five. "I discussed it with a urologist, and he laughed at me," he says. "He told me that he could try to reverse it with microsurgery, but that the sperm were almost certainly not viable. My vasectomy had been done fifteen years earlier, and no one had reported a viable reversal after that amount of time."

He and Sally tried artificial insemination, using a sperm bank in a city about four hundred miles away. "We went through some real experiences, getting this stuff shipped here in a dry ice container," Sam says. "First we had to get in contact with some gynecologists who were into infertility. We found this team of two doctors who were doing all kinds of things like artificial insemination and in-vitro. I did some reading about it and it seemed like it was going to be a piece of cake—you know, putting the right stuff in the right place at the right time. But we tried seven times, and not one took. It turns out to be a crapshoot. You have a one-in-seven chance of getting pregnant each time, and each individual time there are new statistics—the longer it takes, the less of chance there is. It's like witchcraft. No one has the same way of doing it. Some people use fresh sperm, some washed sperm, some concentrated sperm, and there is no standardization on the results."

For almost a year, Sam and Sally tried artificial insemination. They were going crazy dealing with the chemical kit, the urine tests, and the hurried trips down to the lab whenever they got a certain result. Saturday night, Thursday morning, whenever it might be. Then Sally's period would be late one day, two days, three days, and they thought, okay, we're on our way. Then she'd walk out of the bathroom with tears in her eyes and announce that she'd gotten her period.

A new doctor wanted them to go through another set of tests, but it just seemed like a prescription for more frustration. They were discussing what they were going to do next, if anything, when, remarkably, they got a call from a friend who was a nurse and had gone through a midwifery program. She was calling from a clinic in a rural area of the state. She said she had a birth mother who wanted to give them her baby.

They spoke to the birth mother on the phone and she seemed like a nice woman. Then, a few days later, they drove to a town in the middle of the state to see her. They had lunch and met her two young children, who she said were part of the reason she was willing to give up this child. The other part of the reason—and what seemed like the main part—was that she was having problems with her estranged husband, who apparently wasn't the father of the child. They thought the mother was a little "spacey," but she seemed very genuine, so they made an arrangement to help her financially.

But as the pregnancy went on, the stories got more involved. She told them her "boyfriend" was an epileptic and that he hit her. Then she wanted more money and convinced them to give it to her by saying things like, "You want me to eat well and take care of myself, don't you?"

"She turned out to be a druggie," Sam says. "She was on coke and her boyfriend was a biker. Finally, he beat her up one time too many and that caused her to go into labor about a month before she was due. The baby was born prematurely. We went down to see him, and he was in an incubator and then on a respirator. It was very sad."

Not long afterward, the birth mother had second thoughts about giving the child up and put off signing the adoption papers. Then, a few days later, she said no, she definitely didn't want to give the baby up. And just like that, their deal fell through.

"For us, it was a disaster," Sam says. "We thought it was the worst thing that had ever happened to us. We went off very disenchanted—very, very depressed. We honestly did not know where to turn."

A few weeks went by. Then one day Sally met a woman in one of her special education training classes who had adopted a child. After hearing Sally's story, she told her, "You're going about it all wrong," and gave Sally the name of the adoption counselor who had managed her adoption process.

Just as Ted and Sandra had made a brochure to "introduce" themselves, Sam and Sally prepared a letter and pictures which they sent to every registered midwife in the country—more than 1,100 letters.

They got three leads very quickly, one from a midwife in Tampa, Florida, who was counseling a sixteen-year-old girl who wanted to give up her baby. The girl had looked at a lot of pictures and had narrowed it down to two couples, Sam and Sally, and another couple from New Jersey. The second lead was from Phoenix and the third from Portland. But the counselor advised them against pursuing the second and third birth mothers because neither seemed ready to commit, so they focused on the girl from Florida.

They sent letters and pictures back and forth, but suddenly everything stopped. She had picked the other couple. "It was purely arbitary," Sam told us. "It wasn't because I was in my fifties and Sally was almost forty. The other couple was just slightly younger than we were."

They began to feel they weren't destined to be parents. A few days later, though, the adoption counselor called. "This is your fairy godmother calling," she told them, "with some good news and some bad news. The good news is that I've had contact with another birth mother, she is in her eighth month, and the baby is a girl. The bad news is that I don't know where this town in Appalachia is."

They found the town, and Sally spent three weeks living there with the midwife who was counseling the birth mother and who would eventually deliver her baby. The state's laws require that a newborn child remain there for three weeks before being adopted by parents in another state, so Sam and Sally decided to go live with the midwife. "We didn't have to go," Sam says, "but the child was just sitting there, and we wanted to be able to establish a bond from day one. We also wanted to see the area where the birth mother was from. We thought that was somehow important."

Though they never got to meet the birth mother, who just wanted the baby "gone," Sam and Sally established close relations with several people in town and have been able to maintain indirect contact with the birth mother through the midwife.

"The birth mother is not at the point where she wants to have a real dialogue," Sam says. "But we sent her a honey-baked ham for Christmas, and we plan to go back there next spring to visit the midwife and her husband. If the birth mother has a desire to meet us, we'll certainly be there."

The birth mother was only nineteen years old, but to her, Sam's age was never an issue. From the midwife, they learned that she liked the idea that they were doctors and thought that they would give the baby a good life. She was right. Today, Sally is a full-time mother, having given up her private practice, and Sam stays home on Thursdays and weekends to relieve her. He claims to be much more involved this time around than he was with his older kids, whom he "sometimes neglected" because he was going through the rigors of getting started in private practice.

"I really feel very warm inside," he says today, smiling. "She is a cute, wonderful little girl, full of personality. After all we went through, what can I say? She is a tremendously happy ending. When I see her smile, I know it was worth all of it."

OUT $10,000
AND NOTHING TO SHOW FOR IT

Probably the worst nightmare of any adoptive parent is that the birth mother will—days, months, or even years after deciding to give up her child—return and want the child back. In closed adoption, once the baby has been legally turned over to the agency, it is practically impossible for the process to be reversed, although couples still have to pass through a trial period as foster parents. But one of the major drawbacks of open adoption is that a birth mother can change her mind and take the baby back within six months from the day the child is born. There are certain measures you can take to prevent this from happening, but unless you are aware of these steps and are willing to spend the extra money they require, the risk of reversal remains, and can make for a very stressful six months.

One father we spoke to, Steve, was in his mid forties when he tried to have a child with his second wife, a former coworker who was ten years his junior. After several miscarriages, they discovered that she had an anomaly in her reproductive system, and decided to adopt. At the suggestion of a friend, they went to an adoption attorney in town who was "the guy they wanted."

And he didn't disappoint. Within seven months—a relatively short period of time in the adoption game—they had a wonderful baby boy from a seventeen-year-old birth mother who lived in a rural area near the Washington-Idaho border. The attorney had screened the young woman, and she, in turn, had picked Steve and his wife from among the twenty or so prospective parents' brochures the attorney had sent her.

What happened next is fodder for made-for-TV movies.

"We had the child home for about a month when we got a call from our attorney," Steve says. "And he said, I've got some bad news. The birth mother wants her child back."

"What are you talking about?" Steve said. "She can't have her child back. She gave him to us."

"Yes, she can," the lawyer said. "We talked about this before. She has six months to change her mind."

"That's absurd. Isn't there some legal action we can take? She signed papers. We paid for her medical expenses, her legal fees. It just isn't fair."

"I know it isn't," the lawyer said. "But at the same time, it's perfectly within her rights. There's nothing we can do. I wish we could. But we can't. I'm sorry, Steve."

"Can't we talk to her?"

"I suggested that," the lawyer said. "But she doesn't want to talk. She just wants her child back."

"Did she give a reason?"

She had, in fact, given the lawyer a reason, though Steve didn't think much of it. She told the lawyer that the father of the baby, who was nineteen and unemployed, had convinced her that his mother could take care of the child while they found their way back together as a couple.

"Listen," the lawyer said. "After this settles in — after you begin to get over it — we'll talk, and we can try again. I know it's terrible, but it's not the end of the world."

The birth mother indeed took the baby back, and there was absoutely nothing Steve and his wife could do. They had known the risk existed, but that did not dampen the pain when it happened. And if the disappointment of losing a baby wasn't enough, they were also out about $10,000, with nothing to show for it but anger and depression.

But because the attorney was a good one, he quickly made a new birth parent contact for them, and six months after the disaster, they had another baby. This time, to protect themselves against a change of heart, they brought in a local adoption agency to serve as the "transfer agent." The birth parents turned the child over to the agency, and even though they knew who the adoptive parents were, the process had all the legal characteristics of a closed adoption.

Why didn't they take this action with the first baby? Didn't their attorney tell them that the option existed?

"No, he didn't," Steve says. "He only told us after the first mishap. And believe me, we weren't happy about it. We almost got a new attorney."

The reason the attorney gave them for failing to tell them about the option was, "Things aren't normally done that way." Normally, he said, a couple hires a lawyer *or* an adoption agency to act as a finder for a child. But rarely does a couple hire both a lawyer and an agency because of the costs involved.

The lawyer was right. Adopting through lawyers, agencies, and private adoption counselors is expensive — not as expensive as fertility enhancement, but still up there. And the more people you bring in, the more you have to pay.

Another reason the lawyer may not have informed Steve and his wife about the option of bringing in an agency is that adoption lawyers would prefer not to share their fees. Agencies can do much of the legwork connected with adoption, but get paid for that service. And whereas there is some competition between adoption lawyers and agencies, in states where open adoption exists, many agencies are now willing to work with adoption attorneys and other private counselors to conduct home visits before the child to be adopted is born, just as they would in the case of a closed adoption. This is called agency-assisted adoption. Seventy-two hours after the baby is born (the time varies from state to state), the birth mother formally "relinquishes" the baby to the agency, and the prospective adoptive parents formally become the child's foster parents. Again, this is just as if it were a closed adoption.

For this service, the prospective adoptive parents have to pay a fee to both the adoption agency and the lawyer or adoption counselor who acted as a finder and screener of the birth mother and performed other legal services. It is worth it. Adoption is too emotionally complex a process to go into without fielding the best team you can put together, especially when the so-called professional matchmakers working this tricky emotional and financial territory are hardly regulated. The landscape is littered with honest folks who have been taken in by unscrupulous or merely incompetent dream merchants promising babies but not "delivering." In open adoption, the choice of intermediary can make the difference between a happy ending and a disaster.

THE LOGIC OF MIDDLE-AGE ADOPTION

Horror stories aside — and everyone who has adopted knows many of them — open adoption done right is a blessing for late bloomers and the children they adopt. It allows people who cannot conceive to live out their desire to parent a child. Despite the drawbacks of their age, *because* older adoptive parents are already beyond normal childbearing age, they are less likely to consider infertility a curse. Since they know that their chances for starting a biological family are slimmer than most, they don't view creating a family through adoption as a second-best way. For many older adoptive parents, the simple fact that a young mother would even want them to parent her child is in itself a wonderful affirmation of their more mature relationship.

And don't think that it is by chance that young mothers choose older couples. At some level, they must sense that middle-aged, second-marriage couples are more likely to be stable and financially better off than younger parents. They may also sense that middle-aged men have more time to be active fathers. These reasons enable young mothers to justify giving their babies away. It makes their sacrifice seem "right" and good for the baby.

Dan, a middle-aged father who has gone through the vulnerability and self-doubt of meeting with much younger birth mothers over a two-year period, tells us about the affirming power that this act of giving and taking can have for an older man.

"Stacey was born on a Thursday afternoon in May, at two P.M.," he begins. "I didn't know that at the time—had not even met her birth mother in person, although my wife had spent an afternoon with her and I had a long telephone conversation with her the month before. It was all a last-minute, low-probability relationship, with the adoption lawyer giving us little hope of getting this baby, especially if it were a girl. There was too much uncertainty and vacillation by the birth mother about giving up the child.

"On that Thursday afternoon, I was meeting in the office with some clients when my secretary walked into the room and handed me a note. It said simply, 'You have an urgent call. Ms. Hirsch wants you to call her back immediately.' Ms. Hirsch was the adoption attorney. Since I was to have my first meeting with the birth mother the next day in a town about an hour away, I assumed that this call was to cancel the meeting. When I got Ms. Hirsch on the phone in my outer office, she was very excited. 'We have been trying to reach you or your wife at home. You are the father of a baby girl!' I remember I could hear a loud noise. It was air, rushing out of my lungs. Tears came into my eyes. I could not believe what she had said, nor my reaction. I was hysterically happy.

"She explained that the baby had come two weeks early and that our 'iffy' birth mother had definitely decided to go ahead with us. Mother and child were waiting for us at the hospital. I called there, talked to this wonderfully collected young woman who would forever be the reason for my daughter, and then tried frantically to find my wife. Three hours later, we were at the hospital with a five-hour-old baby in our arms, with the mother gazing on from her bed. This was not my baby and it was not my wife's baby. It belonged to the self-assured madonna in the hospital bed taking in our obvious, utter happiness at holding this child. But twelve hours later, it was *our* baby. Hers because she gave it life and ours because we would bring her up to adulthood."

Dan will never forget two things about that day. The first is the look in the birth mother's eyes as she studied his wife's and his reaction to what she had done for them. The second is his wife's radiant face as she held the newborn child. The room was full of complicated emotions—happiness mixed with sadness, thoughts about what others were thinking—and Dan was glad that he had had two years to prepare for them.

"Remember," Dan says, "I had never met the birth mother before I walked into that maternity ward, and I had real misgivings about her reaction to a man over fifty who intended to be the parent of her baby."

Although he wondered what she would be like, he was more afraid of what she would think of him. Maybe he wouldn't pass the test. Maybe she would suddenly decide she had made a terrible mistake. Who was this gray-haired, slightly overweight man who was old enough to be her father? The nerve of him, wanting to be a father.

"But I guess I passed," Dan says. "Because later she told the lawyer that when she saw the looks on our faces, she knew she had done the right thing. My age was never mentioned once, except when I told her over the phone that I was fifty-one."

The more discussions we had with older adoptive fathers, the more we realized that all had greatly overestimated the effect that their age would have on the search for a child. There is John, in his mid sixties—a retired father who stays home with his three-year-old while his wife, Helen, works as a manager for a major corporation. She had three miscarriages and they could not find anything wrong, though she was in her early forties. Rather than force it, they decided to adopt, but they were afraid that with John pushing sixty they were going to have a hard time getting a baby. But through an adoption counselor at an agency that had gone "open," they quickly found a young woman in New England who liked their brochure.

Helen remembers that the first time they called, she and John talked to the young woman and her mother. "We were pretty strict because we wanted absolutely no history of drugs or alcohol or diabetes, and they liked that. They knew we would be good parents. We had a good income and we were not going to get divorced. That made them feel all right about the age part."

John and Helen had everything arranged to go to New England and get the baby as soon as the birth mother left the hospital. But the day the birth mother was supposed to come home, the social worker from the state welfare agency told her that she would have to give the baby into foster care for two weeks, as required by state law.

"The birth mother's grandmother called Helen at the office," John remembers, "and said they didn't want to let the baby go into a foster home. Helen and I were ignorant of the law, but our agency saved the day because they told us to fly the baby, mother, and grandmother out here and they could leave the baby in our foster care. Our agency had worked it out with the authorities back East. So we did it, and they lived with us for five days. It was really something. We took them around and they loved it. The baby stayed with us in the room. We didn't know exactly what to do. We were so scared that if the baby started crying a lot, they would think that we were bad parents. We stayed up all night. At the end, they felt very good about us. They knew we would stay in touch, and we have."

When another couple, Michael and Carrie, went to a well-known adoption lawyer in southern California, they immediately brought up the issue of Michael's age, which was a major concern for them. But the lawyer told them it would not be a problem.

Michael, who is fifty, says, "I knew someone older than me who had adopted, so I realized it could be done. But I confess, if I were placing my child up for adoption, I wouldn't give her to older parents."

He and Carrie went to Louisiana to meet their first birth mother. She herself was almost thirty, unusual for an adoption situation. But she had another child, was not married, and felt that it would be better for this second baby to grow up in another family. She also had a college education and identified with Michael because he was a history professor. "She found out what I did for a living. Her favorite professor in college had been a history professor — a kind of mentor for her, and fortunately she universalized that experience. She thought all history professors were mentor types."

Even so, she wasn't altogether comfortable about his age, maybe because she herself was not so young. Michael thinks her maturity gave her a clearer assessment of the possible problems that could arise for her child with a father his age. The only thing they could do was

say, "Look, come out and see for yourself and get to know us,"
Michael says. So she came to live with them for the last eight weeks of
her pregnancy. If she had doubts, she did not discuss them. At the end
of the two months, she gave birth to a baby girl and Michael and
Carrie were parents.

The story does not end there. Before the birth mother from
Louisiana had come to live with them, Michael and Carrie had been
pursuing a second lead. That had cooled—or so they thought. But
then, just after the birth of their adopted baby, they got a call from the
adoption attorney about the second birth mother. She had definitely
decided that she wanted to give her baby to them. The lawyer told
them that Carrie reminded this birth mother so much of a close cousin
whom she admired that she had rejected nineteen other couples' fold-
ers in favor of theirs.

Michael looks down and shakes his head as he thinks about their
reaction. "We never imagined adopting two children at once. We
thought we were going for one, and then three years later we would
try again if successful this time. When it became apparent that we
could really have two, we decided that it would be ridiculous to pass
this chance up. Our life experience taught us both to seize opportunities. So we did it."

Michael had another reason to want to adopt a second child. In
his previous, twenty-five-year-long marriage, he had one daughter,
now in her early thirties. He feels that she would have had a better
time of it had she been one of two or three children. "I was very sensitive to her 'onlyness,'" he explains. "On the other hand, when you
have two young children, it's very difficult to read a book at night. If
we manage to stay up past nine-thirty, we can't read more than a page
before we pass out. The kids are up at six or earlier, so it's hard. One
of the things I was right about, though, is that having 'almost twins' is
easier because they always have a companion. They play a lot together and are great friends."

IS IT MORAL FOR OLDER COUPLES TO ADOPT?

In the old days, when agencies controlled the adoption market, older
parents were deemed unsuitable and therefore excluded from becoming adoptive parents. The very rich and famous could always find babies to adopt through direct connections, but "ordinary" older
couples had to go overseas. Those efforts usually also meant dealing
with agencies. At best, older couples would be able to find a two- or

three-year-old child who needed a foster home and then would be eligible for adoption. The risk of adopting a child with deep-seated problems was that much greater, although for most children a loving and stable home can cure a lot of past troubles.

Now that the adoption possibilities for middle-aged folks have changed, the opposite is happening. Older couples who want to parent usually have more resources and stability than younger couples. They may look better to a birth mother wanting to place her unborn child in a situation that she might have always wanted for herself. They can make themselves look attractive in a marketplace that has no higher judge than individual tastes—no agencies making moral decisions on what is good and not good for adopted babies.

Many Americans agree with this free market philosophy. It is consistent with American values of individual rights and consistent with the majority's view of privacy: Women should be able to make the decision, without external interference, of who should raise their child. In adoptions, the child and birth mother are even protected by state laws requiring that foster parents be screened by an approved agency and then undergo further screening before becoming the child's legal guardians.

Mother decides she likes older parents, they are approved by a state-regulated agency, and everyone is happy. So, what's the problem? There are always questions: Is not the relationship between adoptive parents and adopted children complicated enough without having advanced-middle-aged adoptive parents? And is there not a higher order of morality than the marketplace to tell us whether something is right or wrong?

Most people will tell you that they do not like the idea of young women giving up their kids to men in their fifties. Add in the middle-aged Europeans and Americans running around Third World countries looking to adopt, and it smacks of the rich buying children from the poor, of old gringos grabbing up babies from the oppressed and downtrodden. And since a majority of the trades in the open (and closed) adoption market are from lower-income mothers to much higher-income adoptive parents, you don't have to stretch your imagination much to see that the stereotype is not far off from what is actually going on.

We found two typical responses to this dilemma among older adoptive fathers. The first is that they *do* worry about not being around long enough, but feel that the benefits to their adopted children, to their wives, who otherwise would have been childless, and to themselves outweigh the negative of being around for only fifteen to twenty years. Michael tells us that a chance phone call in the middle of his adoption process greatly affected his own thinking about the age problem. "I was worried about bringing up a baby only to leave the scene too early, and thought that maybe I was doing the wrong thing, when a psychologist I met at a party the week before happened to call me. I don't know why he bothered, but something I said to him about the adoption must have triggered an instinctual understanding that I was vascillating. When he called, he recounted that when he was born, his own father was about my age, and that his father died fourteen years later. But their relationship was so wonderful and happy that he had no resentment toward his father at all. True, the man had died early. But the psychologist cherished those fourteen years so much that they carried him through whatever he had to face in his twenties and thirties."

After that call, Michael figured that he would just focus on having the closest possible relationship with his adopted children over the next fifteen years, and should that be the end of his time, he would leave them with the same kind of legacy the psychologist's father had left him.

A close friend of ours, who had adopted a baby when he was fifty and his (second) wife was forty, took a somewhat different tack, yet came to the same conclusion. "We went through a lot of heartache for three years before we found our son," he says. "The losses hit us hard —infertility and miscarriages, then an 'almost' adoption that fell apart. It was all very painful, but also involving in a way that pregnancy as a young father usually is not. When I was in my twenties and my wife got pregnant, it was exciting—and easy. I remember the day she went to the gynecologist for the rabbit test. My heart bounced when she told me the results. I was proud and happy. The whole thing was natural, effortless; yes, emotional, but hardly time-consuming and barely involving. Especially if you didn't want to make it your life's work.

"The struggle of the second time around was very different. I had to be absorbed. Every time I thought having a family would take care of itself, I was made to take an active role. It demanded effort, discussion, decision. It was sometimes exhilarating, but often painful. This time, creating a family had become my main job."

Our friend believes that the drawn-out, collective effort to "make parenting happen" not only transformed him from just taking responsibility for the family into a "child-bearer," but resolved his dilemma about becoming a father again at the age of fifty. He felt that he could give his adopted child more than men who had not gone through this process.

"Women often complain that they are the ones who biologically have to carry the child, and that this allows men a major separation from the birth process," he explains. "When conception ceases to be a matter of course, the man is drawn in much more forcefully. Is it his problem that is the cause of all these difficulties? What should we as a couple do? Do we really want to go through all this? Why not just lead a childless life? Think about all the advantages of being adults on our own. I never had to ask any of these questions in my first marriage—either about our goals as a couple or about ourselves *in* the couple. As young marrieds in those days, we assumed we would be normal, upward bound, ambitious, accumulative strivers with two children, a house, and two cars. And it just happened. No self-examination, no long discussions, no hitches, no crises that bonded us, and no insights about that thing called family life and our individual roles in it. When real choices have to be made, that changes. It sure changed me and the way I felt about this adopted baby. She would never be taken for granted. I knew that and I knew that whatever time I had with her—even if it were only fifteen years—would be something that would give her a special strength as an adult."

Although these self-justifications for adoption by older men (and women) are self-serving, there is a ring of truth to them. Perhaps the market is morally right in this respect, and the agencies that judged older parents as unsuitable were morally wrong.

There is one more point to consider. Adopted children not only have their adoptive parents; complicated as that relation may be, they also have their natural parents. Open adoption makes it possible for birth mothers (and fathers) to keep in touch with their child's adoptive family, if they choose to. They know exactly where their child is and the name of the adoptive parents. That is what open adoption is about. Some open adoptions are even "co-op adoptions," where the adoptive parents and the birth mother maintain a kind of partial joint custody of the adopted child.

For example, Alan and Patricia adopted their son, Josh, seven years ago and take him back East once a year to see his birth mother. Patricia, herself an adoptee, pushed for this arrangement because of her own identity crisis as she grew into adulthood without knowing her natural parents. It was only in her twenties that she finally found her birth mother, and she never forgot what it meant to have that connection. For better or worse, Patricia and Alan want Josh to get a sense of who he is across the entirety of his parentage. Another adoptive couple we know who live nearer the birth mother have her over for dinner every two weeks. Their child is growing up with one set of parents and a second mother.

Although it may seem strange in our society to do things this way, many older couples feel good about maintaining contact with the birth mother, if not quite to a "co-op" level, at least to sending pictures, exchanging letters, and sharing their experiences. If the birth mother accepts this arrangement—and understandably the pain of separation and guilt makes many unwilling to—it does create an "extended family" for the adopted child that buffers the advanced age of adoptive parents.

However, it should be noted that there is resistance to open adoption. The director of a national adoption organization, interviewed on National Public Radio,[4] criticized open adoption because it seemed to assume that the adoption process was never over—not for adoptive parents or birth mother or adoptee—and therefore served mainly to employ psychologists and social workers to counsel the different parties for years to come.

One parent analyzed this resistance to nonagency adoption as emerging from an old-fashioned morality. "The pregnant woman who avoids the agency route is seen as unrepentant for daring to hold on to a modicum of autonomy despite her 'fallen' posture," Paul Tick wrote in *Genesis* 2, a Jewish publication out of Cambridge, Massachusetts. "The adoptive parents, afforded the opportunity to interact with the birth mother, to give emotional support and help her feel positive about her birthing and surrendering of the baby, are seen as mercenary, stiff-necked, refusing to accept Fate's judgment upon them as infertile. Private adoption, in other words, is not a morality play that reinforces the parties' conditions of helplessness—it is a deal worked out to alter those conditions. By most standards, this is threatening and unacceptable."[5]

Threatening or not, open adoption has been a boon to older couples. But with all its pitfalls and uncertainties, doing it right makes it a lot less intimidating and gives adoptive parents a considerably higher chance of success.

6

. . . .

In the Shadows: The Other Children

From a very early age, parents push their children into new and different situations that they are not comfortable with. A father stands by the edge of a playground, encouraging his three-year-old daughter to go play with the other children, but she is shy and does not want to. So he picks her up and places her in the sandbox next to the other children and says, "Go ahead, play, there's nothing to be afraid of." Terrified, she begins to cry, but in a matter of moments the tears are gone: She has found a friend and is playing happily, digging in the sand with a plastic shovel.

"See," her father says on the way home, "that wasn't so bad now, was it?"

As the years pass, she hears him say this time and time again. After her first day of school, after her first piano recital, after he changes jobs and she has to move to a new town and make new friends. But in the end, everything seems to turn out all right. Like a piece of wood that's thrown into the water, she sinks at first, but always surfaces. And after she weathers each ordeal, her father says, "See, that wasn't so bad, was it?"

He believes that his daughter, like most human beings — like him, in fact — can and will be able to get used to anything. But one day that faith is tested. He and his wife — his daughter's mother — have decided to divorce. Not only does he wonder whether he will be able to get used to that, but he wonders whether his daughter will. He asks his divorced friends how their children are coping with their divorces and they say things like, "It's tough at first, but they get used to it."

And sure enough, although there are some painful scenes, she grows accustomed to the situation, and before long a new order is established. It is not necessarily a perfect order, but it's one that she seems able to live with.

But one day that order is shattered. Her father is getting remarried, and she is devastated. "Why her?" she asks. "What's so great about her that you have to get married?"

"We get along well," he says. "She's good for me."

"So what," she says. "You got along with a lot of other women. How come you didn't marry them?"

He does not say anything. But in his silence, he thinks, "It's going to be tough at first, but she'll get used to it."

And sure enough, he's right. Gradually, daughter and stepmother start to get along with each other, or at least respect each other's positions. And once again, a new order is established. But Dad is not finished. Soon he's ready to upset that order again. But this time it's the coup de grace. The world rocker.

"Your stepmother and I are thinking of having a child," he announces one day.

And what does his daughter say? She says, "That really sucks."

After that, Dad decides he should not bring up the topic anymore. And while he is a little worried about what will happen when the child is born, he is fairly certain his daughter's attitude will change over time. After all, she has been able to get used to everything he has done so far, so why should she not be able to get used to this?

Chances are she will. But until now little has been written about how the grown children of a father's first marriage feel about his having more children. While the media have focused on the ethics and experience of becoming a father at a more advanced age, the opinions of the older children — or, as we call them sometimes, the "first" children — have been virtually ignored. When first children are mentioned, they tend to be footnotes to their ages, used primarily for shock value. "Bill Erikson has one child who is thirty and another who is two," a typical article will read. But Bill's thirty-year-old child is almost never quoted.

Part of the reason first children have been ignored in the media is that older fathers themselves ignore them, or at least, do not allow them to carry much weight in their decision-making. Take the testimony of Jeremy Hamand, whose first-person account of being an older father appeared in the English newspaper *The Independent* in 1993:

I didn't really think about how the [older] children would react to the new baby—would not have decided against having a baby to save the feelings of my older children. I wanted to have children with Maggie and I knew she wanted them. Intellectually, I knew there would be problems. You have to be aware of the feelings that are going on, but beyond that there's not much you can do. You have to be sensitive about how you treat your older children; but even when you are, it may not be enough. I don't think there's any clean way of doing these things, but as children get older it becomes easier.

Hamand, like our generic father above, believes time is the only real healer. Eventually, they will get used it. We spoke to many older fathers who felt the same way. And while they were concerned about the feelings of their first children, they did not think they should be handcuffed by them.

"It would be one thing if my son and daughter were ten and eleven and living with me," one man tells us. "Then I might be more concerned about what they thought and how it might affect them. But now that they are grown and living off on their own, I feel they have as much of a right to interfere with my life as I have a right to interfere with theirs. They can say what they want and be angry, but I'm not going to let that prevent me from doing something I want and need to do."

"I don't have a problem with that," his twenty-eight-year-old son says. "But I do think he should make an effort to tell us what's going on and explain why he's doing what he's doing, so it doesn't come as a big surprise. I think the problem is he knows we're not going to be happy about some of this stuff so he just doesn't tell us until he really has to. But when he does that we lose respect for him because we think he has no spine."

Herein lies a major conflict between an older father and his first children. What should he tell them and when should he tell? Unfortunately, there seems to be no set formula. An early confession does not guarantee acceptance; nor does a last-minute one necessarily spell doom.

"I only found out my father was going to have another child when he told me his wife was four months pregnant," says Jane, twenty-seven. "But I'm not sure it would have made that much of a difference if I found out earlier. I still would have had to deal with the question of who my family was. That's the first thing you're confronted with, this changing notion of who your family is, was, and is going to be. It all starts there."

WHO IS FAMILY?

For as long as she could remember, Jane defined her family as her mother, father, brother, and her parents' relatives. Even after her parents divorced when she was twelve, and her father, ten years later, married a woman he had been dating for a couple of years, the definition remained the same. She called her father's wife by her first name, Leslie, and did not think of her as her stepmother. To Jane, she was just "Leslie, my dad's wife."

One summer, Jane went with her father and Leslie to visit Leslie's family in Michigan. Leslie came from a big family, and Jane found herself being introduced to a whole new clan. All in all, they were very nice people, if not exactly the type she was accustomed to. Jane and her brother had grown up in New York City riding the subway; these people had grown up in a small town driving pickup trucks. While Jane was graduating from an Ivy League university, her step-cousins were on their way to large state universities or small midwestern colleges she had never heard of. But they still had things in common. They listened to similar music, liked the same movies, and enjoyed camping and waterskiing.

"I had a good time," she says. "But after the week was over, I didn't feel any more related to these people than before. I showed my vacation pictures to a couple of friends and they kept asking, 'who's he?' or 'who's she?' And for convenience sake I would say, 'Oh, that's my stepcousin.' But I really thought they were just relatives of my father's wife that I had hung out with for a few days."

Her father was forty-eight when he married Leslie, who was thirty-six and childless. After the wedding, Jane asked her father whether he planned to have children with his new wife, and he said no, because Leslie could not — or rather, it would be dangerous for her to try. When Leslie was a teenager, he explained, she had a kidney removed. After the operation, the doctors told her she would be taking a big risk having a baby.

"On a certain level I felt bad for her because I was a woman and wouldn't want that to happen to me," Jane says. "But at the same time, I felt relieved. And I think my father sensed that." She remembered him saying, "Don't worry, kid, you and your brother are it for me."

But three years later, when she found out Leslie was pregnant, that statement seemed like a bald-faced lie. She was so shocked and angry that she did not speak to her father for almost two months, not until her brother, Paul, told her to lighten up. Her brother had a better attitude about the pregnancy. But Jane thought that was because he was living on the other side of the country, in Seattle, and did not have to deal with his father's antics on a day-to-day or even on a weekly basis.

"He could keep his distance," she says. "Which is the way he wanted it. But I lived and worked in New York and had a closer relationship with our father."

Leslie's pregnancy was not without complications. When the baby, a girl, was born (by cesarian section), she arrived six weeks premature and had to be put in an incubator. Although Leslie was doing well, for several days the child's life hung in the balance. While Jane hoped the baby would survive, a couple of times she found herself thinking, "Well, it wouldn't be so awful if she died," which, in turn, brought on feelings of guilt.

Those first few weeks were a roller-coaster ride for Jane. One moment she was relieved the child's condition was improving, and in the next she was thinking about how her being born was going to affect her life. For so long, it had just been her and her brother; suddenly, there was this other person, this innocent little baby, who was screwing up the whole picture.

During that period, Jane spent a lot of time talking to her mother, who was living just outside the city in Westchester County, and did not mind telling Jane that her father was crazy for starting a second family. Her mother was not as upset about it as Jane, but she understood what Jane was going through and did not push her to hurry up and get over her bitterness. "That's all I really wanted," Jane says. "I just wanted someone to tell me it was okay to be bitter."

The thing that bothered her the most was that because of this baby — her name was Nicole — she had suddenly become forever attached to Leslie's relatives in Michigan. Whereas before they were just Leslie's relatives, now they were her relatives, too; Nicole was as much a part of their family as she was a part of hers. That was a fact.

"That's true," Jane's father told her. "But that's not the worst thing in the world. I mean, someday you'll get married, and you'll inherit a whole other family from your husband. Some of those people you'll like and some of them you won't."

"I know," Jane said. "But at least I'll have chosen the family. At least I'll have been the one in control."

"There are many things you can't control," her father said.

Jane agreed, but it did not make her feel any better. She says, "I had to get over the feeling that I was somehow responsible for what had taken place. In that sense, there are some similarities to a divorce situation. You think, hey, my father managed to bring up two pretty good kids. We didn't get involved in drugs or end up living at home after college and being freeloaders. I mean, we're reasonably successful, so he must have done something right. But then he goes ahead and does something like this and you wonder, hey, maybe I did something wrong. If you don't have that strong a relationship with your father to begin with, getting over that doubt is tough. It really is."

TO PARTICIPATE, OR NOT TO PARTICIPATE: THAT IS THE QUESTION

Inevitably, the arrival of a new sibling, whether blood-related or not (in the case of adoption), presents the offspring of a father's first marriage with the choice of whether or not to become active participants in their father's new family. Often, the choice is dictated by circumstances. Many offspring of a father's first marriage, especially those in their late twenties or early thirties, already lead very separate lives from their parents and may even have families of their own. For instance, Jane's brother, Paul, who is thirty and writes for an educational television show in Seattle, speaks with his father once a month and sees him once a year. They have neither a close nor distant relationship, he says. Rather, they have an understanding. "He doesn't tell me what to do and I don't tell him what to do," Paul says. And as things stand, they get along pretty well.

"For the most part in recent years, my attitude has been, whatever makes you happy, Dad," Paul tells us. "I've stopped trying to understand why he was dating certain women or why he ended up marrying whom he did. That's his business. If he wants to have another kid, then he should have another kid. If that's what makes him happy, then he should do it. I mean, it'd be very easy for me to say that what he's done is crazy — why would he want to put an additional burden on himself? But I don't know what's it like to be fifty. Who knows, I may want to have a kid when I'm fifty."

Nicole's arrival did nothing to change Paul's decision not to play an active role in his father's life. Maybe someday, he says, he will develop a bond with his halfsister, but as it is, he sees her too infrequently to feel strongly about her one way or the other.

Jane, on the other hand, has grown more accepting of "the situation," as she calls it, and today, fifteen months after Nicole was born, she is a frequent baby-sitter at her father's apartment. She says she owes her change of heart to a number of factors, including Leslie's patience and sensitivity. In the end, however, she simply decided she wanted to remain part of her father's life.

"In the years leading up to Nicole's birth, I'd really put a lot of effort into having a closer my relationship with my father," she says. "I finally decided that I didn't want to let all that effort go to waste. It took a while for me to come to that conclusion, but now that I have, I feel better about Nicole. She's also a good kid. That helped, too."

UNFORGIVEN

At almost the same time that Jane's half sister, Nicole, was struggling for her life in an incubator in a New York City hospital, two thousand miles away, in Austin, Texas, another child was being born. His name was Benjamin, and he was the son of Michael, a physicist and project manager at a computer company, and Dana, an editor at a university press. Dana, at thirty-four, was a first-time mother; Michael, at fifty-one, became a father for the third time.

The first person Michael called was his mother, who was not exactly thrilled by the news. "I hope you know what you're doing, Michael," she said.

Next he called his daughter, Vivian, twenty-two, who worked for a politician.

"You have a baby brother," he told her.

"Half brother," she corrected him.

"Half brother," he said.

"Just do me a favor, Dad. Don't make me come and see him right away, Okay? Don't make a big deal out of it. I'll come and see him when I'm ready."

"Okay."

"Have you talked to Brian yet?"

Brian was her older bother.

"I thought I'd wait," he said.

"Don't wait, Dad. He's not going to be happy either way. But if you wait, it'll be worse. Now he just thinks you have poor judgment. If you wait, he'll think you're a coward, too."

"Don't worry, I'll call him," he said.

But he did not—not right away. First he called some people who he knew would be congratulatory—his good friend Charles and a couple of colleagues from work. Only when he got home later that evening did he finally talk to his son.

"I just wanted to let you know you that Dana gave birth to a seven-pound, four-ounce baby boy this morning," he said.

"I suppose he had to come out sometime," Brian said.

"Yes, that's what usually happens."

"Well, you asked for it, now you've got it. I hope you're happy."

"Right now, I'm pretty tired. It was a long night. I just wanted to let you know."

"I appreciate it," his son said sarcastically.

"We'll talk soon, okay?"

"Yeah, sure. Maybe between diaper changes."

Michael laughed awkwardly, not knowing quite how to respond. "Well, when things get settled," he said after a moment, "we'll have you and your sister over."

"Whatever you say, Dad."

Although he ignored his son's wisecrack at the time, Michael found himself thinking about it later. He knew that Brian was taking two jabs at him at once. While on one level Brian was saying, "Between diapers and the kid, you're not really going to have time for me, are you?" he was also saying, "Hey, maybe you'll actually get around to changing a diaper this time around."

Had he been so terrible to his children? He did not think so, but he also knew that they did not seem to see it that way. And what was worse, they were not going to let him forget it.

"He's right we aren't going to let him forget it," Vivian tells us a little over a year after her half brother was born. "That's like my father's solution to everything: Maybe they'll forget. Maybe it'll slip their mind. He wishes everybody was like Ronald Reagan without the Republican rhetoric. That would be his ideal world."

She says his maybe-they'll-forget defense dates back to the years just following his divorce, but became more prevalent in the months just prior to his second marriage, when she brought up the possibility of his having more children. Dana, his live-in girlfriend, had expressed a desire to have children, and it seemed clear to Vivian, at least, that if her father wanted to stay with her he was going to have to have a child with her.

"When she gives you the ultimatum, Dad, what are you going to do?" Vivian asked him one day.

Her father just shrugged his shoulders and smiled. "I don't

know," he said. "Maybe it was a passing fancy. Maybe she'll forget about it."

He was joking, but on a certain level, Vivian thought he was serious. That was his answer. That is what bought him time. Maybe she will forget. Vivian did not buy it, of course, and assumed that her father would succumb to his girlfriend's demands, marry her, and have another child. Actually, having that happen did not bother her as much as having her father avoid the issue.

When Vivian was fourteen, her father left her mother for one of the secretaries at his company and never really explained to Vivian or her brother what was going on. He just said things like, "Things didn't work out for your mother and me. It's not your fault." Then he would show up on weekends and act as though things were normal. Vivian and Brian hated that. But while Vivian was not quite sure how she felt about her father's having another child, Brian was dead-set against it from the beginning and told his father to expect "a lot of animosity" if he went through with it.

Brian has not let his father forget that declaration. In fact, he was so upset about his half brother's birth that he declined to be interviewed for this book. "He's really having a hard time with it," Vivian says. "I think it just brings up a lot of stuff in him and it's just too painful to talk about. To him, the child is a constant reminder of the divorce. So is the fact that Ben is being brought up by two parents. It's not like we did not have both our parents bringing us up when we were that age, but I still think it makes him jealous."

Another source of resentment is the money his father is spending —and will have to continue spending on Benjamin. Neither Vivian nor Brian are working at a high-paying job. Vivian is an administrative assistant in a state senator's office and Brian is a freelance journalist. They do not expect their father to supplement their incomes. But it bothers them—Brian especially—that now that their dad is more comfortable financially and might have been able to give them money, his income is used to support his new wife, who has stopped working, and Ben. Brian has also pointed out that their inheritance— "if there's anything left"—will now have to be split three ways instead of two. And if their father decides to have more children, their percentage will dwindle even further.

"When we were growing up, our father always seemed like he was strapped for cash," Vivian says. "He's not rich now, but he's certainly comfortable, especially when his wife is working. It's unclear when she's going to start up again, but I can tell you she still manages to spend a lot of money. And that ticks my brother off, because our mother always worked and was always really careful about what she spent."

Were there other reasons her attitude toward Ben was different from her brother's?

"Well, I think the main difference between my brother and me is that at a certain point I came to the realization that no matter how much I protested, my voice really didn't matter."

And whereas her brother views his half brother's birth as just another contribution to the never-ending rip-off, Vivian sees it as a chance for her father to redeem himself. And she is not shy about telling him that or giving him advice about his marriage. "I have a vested interest in seeing his marriage go well. I don't want to see him get divorced again. And I don't want to see this child grow up in a divorced family. It's not like I want to know how his sex life's going, but I do talk to him about how his marriage is going."

She often finds herself comparing her mother's post-divorce life to her father's. Like her father, her mother is remarried and settled, but for several years after the divorce, she struggled both professionally and personally. Her father, on the other hand, never spent a significant amount of time alone. He was always with someone. Ultimately, however, she thinks the struggle helped her mother grow as a person. "My mother's come a long way," she says. "Her relationship with her husband is very good. And although my father got his ears bent by the 1990s fathering thing and his wife insists he do some work, he's still fumbling around, making a lot of the same mistakes he made when he was younger. He's still not as sensitive to people's needs as he should be."

A WELCOME ADDITION

Pete, twenty-eight, has a different story to tell. Five years ago, when his father's wife, Cheryl, went into labor, he drove her and his father, Dennis, to the hospital.

"When I drove Cheryl to the hospital, it was me, my father, and my cousin," he says. "And we all went into the hospital at the same time—these three guys and this one pregnant woman. Any one of us could have been the father. And the nurse looked at me and was like, 'Are you the father?' And my father said, 'No, I am. That's the brother. And that's the cousin.' We all started laughing."

Pete was not the least bit perturbed by the idea that his father was going to have another child. Nor was his older brother, John. In fact, he says they were basically looking forward to it. But he adds that that might have been because they had a particularly good relationship with their father and his wife before she got pregnant.

"Although my brother and I grew up with our mother after our parents divorced, we both went to work for our father and Cheryl after college. We'd been with them for about a year when Cheryl got pregnant."

The day Pete drove them to the hospital, Dennis was forty-seven and Cheryl was thirty-four. They had been living together for almost ten years and been married for three, but never planned to have a baby because Cheryl had been told by doctors she would not be able to have children.

"When I found out she was pregnant, I was shocked," Pete says. "But it wasn't like I was upset or angry. I was just shocked. She wasn't supposed to have children. They had been together for years, and nothing had happened, and then one day, boom, she's pregnant. I think everybody was a little shocked, but we were all happy for her. I mean, it was sort of a miracle."

Pete says he had actually thought about his father having more children before Cheryl got pregnant, but he never imagined Cheryl would be the mother. "My father is in the garment business so he travels to the Orient a lot," he says. "Because of that I always thought there was some kid out there with an Irish last name and a cleft in his chin who I didn't know about. I pictured myself going to Hong Kong and running into someone who looked a lot like me but had straight black hair."

When Pete went to L.A. to work for his father after college, things went well almost from the start. The business prospered and Pete ending up getting back together with his high school sweetheart, who also happened to be living in L.A. "We were like one big family out there," Pete says. "Maybe that's why I was looking forward to my father having another child. It just seemed nice. Another addition to the family."

But after that wonderfully crazy day, when father, son, and cousin escorted Cheryl into the hospital, things would never be quite the same for the family business. "After my sister, Katie, was born," Pete says, "the business slowly went downhill. And it wasn't a coincidence. My father was always good with the big picture but not with details. He was an entrepreneur, a salesman who could pitch with the best of them. Cheryl was the one who kept the records and made sure the showroom was in order. She was the one who was good at the details. But little by little, she began to lose her focus on the business. Little by little, she began to spend more time at home with Katie and less time at the office."

By the time Katie was three years old, the business had failed and the family split up: Dennis, Cheryl, and Katie moved to Vermont, John stayed in L.A., and Pete moved back to New York, where he got a job at a large clothing company and married his high school sweetheart. Today, the two live in Brooklyn, not far from Pete's mother.

"My mother doesn't have a lot of good things to say about my father," he says. "But that's all right. I'm glad I went out there. I'm glad I got to be with my father when Katie was born. I learned a lot, watching someone close to me go through that experience. I'm also glad I was able to get to know my sister from such a young age. My wife is glad, too. We're very close to her now."

But like most offspring of a father's first marriage, Pete often finds himself comparing the way he was brought up to the way his father and his wife are bringing up the new child. For many first children, these comparisons can be a source of great resentment, especially if their father is spending more time and money on his second set of children than he did with his first. However, Pete said the difference between his father today and twenty years ago is almost imperceptible. He still has his up and down periods, so his money situation has not changed. And he only spends slightly more time with Katie than he did with Pete and John when they were growing up.

"Because my father didn't have a steady job when we were growing up, he was able to spend a lot of time with us when we lived together," Pete says. "I remember him coaching our baseball teams and taking us to boy scout meetings. He seemed to have time for everything."

Where Pete found a difference was in the way Cheryl was bringing up Katie and the way his mother raised his brother and him. As he remembers it, his mother had a relatively easy time with them. She allowed them a fair amount of freedom, but knew just when to put her foot down. Cheryl, on the other hand, does not give Katie any space and seems to dote on her far more than "a normal parent would." That creates problems when it comes time for Dennis to take care of Katie. She expects the royal treatment and Dennis just does not have the patience to give it to her.

Although he says it is not his place to voice his criticisms to his father or Cheryl, Pete does take careful note as to what he thinks his father and Cheryl are doing wrong, and asks his wife to remind him not to do those things when they have children. "I'm sure we're going to make mistakes, too," he says. "But if what they say is true, that we inherit a lot of our parenting from our parents, then I feel I have an advantage because I've been able to see my father from a couple of different perspectives. While I've been able to see him as my father, I've also been able to see him as a father to someone else at an age when I'm preparing to become a father myself. That can be very enlightening. I can also see how it might make you angry. Honestly, though, I don't harbor any resentment toward my father because he's had this child. If there's anything I hold against him it's the fact that I'm still in the garment business. Things could be worse, but I think both my brother and I would rather be doing something else."

The only other regret he has is not being able to introduce Katie to his mother back in Brooklyn. "When you become close to someone like Katie, whom you think of as your sister, you want the person you are closest to—your mother—to meet her and get to know her. But so far my mother hasn't been too into that idea."

We heard similar comments from other first children who had positive experiences with their younger half siblings and wanted to introduce them to their mothers. But only one young man, Chris, actually took the brave step of bringing his two-year-old half sister over to his mother's house one afternoon without advance warning. "I wanted to show my mother this little person who was going to be a very important thing in my life," Chris says. "I don't know how I expected her to react, but it turned out to be a fairly disappointing experience. When I took my little sister over there, my mother was talking to a friend and ended up kind of brushing me off. She said to her friend, 'This is my ex-husband's kid, can you believe it?' She just didn't want to deal with the situation, which kind of hurt."

Most of the first wives we spoke to were not involved with their children's new half siblings, nor did they want to be. One first wife says, "My daughter asked me whether I was curious about her father's new child—she thought I would be—and I told her, no, I really wasn't. But if she really wanted me to meet him, I'd do that for her. But she had to understand that I wouldn't have any attachment for him. I would look at him and think he was cute and all because I like children. But that was it. After that, I told her, I would want to spend time with her, not with him."

When we tell Pete about Chris's attempt to introduce his half sister to his mother, he laughs and says, "I can see my mother doing something like that. I'm sure she'd be pissed if I brought Katie over unannounced. But I'm going to do it someday. I will, you'll see. She's just going to have to deal with it. I did, so why shouldn't she?"

TEN YEARS DOWN THE ROAD

In the three previous stories, the first children we interviewed were in their twenties and had half siblings who were under five years old. In all those interviews, we asked the first children what they thought their relationships to their half siblings would be like ten or even twenty years down the road. Here's what they said:

JANE: "I don't know if I'll ever be able to think of Nicole as my real sister. But I do think I'll always be close to her."

VIVIAN: "I don't see myself as being a sister or mother to Ben. I'd just like to be a friend."

PETE: "My father jokes that when Katie becomes old enough to date boys, he'll be too old to intimidate her dates, so I'll have to. Even so, I don't see myself becoming a father figure. I really am a brother. I tease her and stuff like a brother would. And the truth is, you'd be surprised how easy it is to act like you're twelve years old."

It would be interesting to be able to interview Jane, Vivian, and Pete ten years down the road and compare their feelings now with their feelings then. Although we won't be able to do that, we did interview six first children who are in their late thirties and early forties who had half siblings who were teenagers or approaching their teen years.

Of the six, four said their relationship with their father and half siblings had not really changed over the years.

"I haven't been close to my father for a number years," one man says. "He lives in Florida, I live in Colorado. So I was never close to his second family. We've met, we know each other, but we lead completely separate lives, and that hasn't changed over the years." Another man says he has always been close to his half siblings because he lives in the same city as his father. "I can't say I'm really a brother, though. I was thirty and married when the first child was born, so I've always felt more like an uncle. It's funny, because my relationship to them is very similar to my uncle's relationship to them. We're both sort of benevolent uncles."

The two people who say their relationships with their half siblings have changed over the years think it has changed as a direct result of a major event. In Peggy's case, it was her own divorce at thirty-five, and in Dan's case, it was the death of his father. Both cases are worth examining more closely.

A CHILD OF DIVORCED PARENTS DIVORCES

"I'm someone whose thinking about my half brothers has changed a lot over the years," Peggy says, sitting in the living room of her Manhattan apartment, which she shares with her German shepherd, Theo. A petite blonde who wears her hair pulled back in a ponytail, she appears conservative, but once the interview starts, it quickly becomes clear she is a fast-talking, straight-shooting New Yorker. And why not? She is a contract negotiator for a firm that sells television broadcast rights.

"In the beginning," she says, "I didn't feel strongly one way or the other about them. My only concern was that my father would have a girl because I had a younger sister who died of leukemia when I was eleven and it just would have bothered me if he had a girl. But then he had a boy, and I was relieved. That's all I really cared about."

Four years later, her father had another boy, but Peggy rarely saw either child because she was living in France. However, when the older boy, Bradley, was six, and the younger boy, Cameron, was two, she got married and moved back to New York. "Obviously, there was some change when I moved back to New York because I actually got to spend some time with these children and establish a relationship. But I think the real change took place three years later, when I started to have problems with my marriage and eventually got divorced."

She pauses a moment, then continues:

"In my twenties and early thirties, I wasn't that dependent on my parents. But when I was going through my divorce, which was a devastating experience, I found myself really leaning on them. They were extremely supportive. My father, who is a lawyer, took care of everything from a legal standpoint. And my mother was terrific. This is going to sound weird, but she really sympathized with me after what she went through with my father."

Ever since that time, Peggy has played a much more active role in her father's second family. A cynic might say that is because she herself, at thirty-eight, is childless and wants to be a mother, but Peggy says it is not as simple as that.

"I would like to be a mother. But I think it's been more of a quid pro quo on my part. As my father gets older, he's beginning to depend on me a lot more for things, and I feel that after he helped me get through some hard times, it's my duty to be supportive. Recently, for instance, he's had some financial problems, and I've had to help him deal with that. If he were on his own, it would be one thing, but it gets more complicated when he's got two boys — one nine, the other thirteen — to raise. You start to feel responsible for them. They're part of the equation."

She says that her father's financial difficulties have put a strain on his marriage, and, like Vivian, she feels a need to protect her half brothers from their parents' marital problems.

"As a child of divorced parents, I think you're a lot more attuned to the problems your father might be having with his marriage. But someone like me, who's been divorced herself, I'm hypersensitive because I've seen it from both perspectives. I also have this fear that when these children grow up they're going to say to me, 'You were there, you were an adult, why didn't you do something?' "

Ultimately, however, she feels her biggest contribution to her half brothers' futures could be a monetary one.

"I've started to put money aside for their college education because I don't know if my father will be around then or if he'll be able to afford it. People say to me, what do you mean, you feel like you have to put them through college? They have a mother. Well, I don't count their mother. It's strange. I just don't count her when it comes to sending them to college and stuff. She works, but we're not talking big money. She comes from a different background than I do and I don't mean that in a snotty way. It's just the way it is. She's more middle-class. She was my father's secretary."

Peggy also has an older brother, Seth, who is forty-one and has two children of his own. They are, ironically, almost identical in age to his father's second set of children. Although he lives outside of Philadelphia, Seth brings his family up to New York about once every six weeks to see his father and his family. The two sets of children play together and often joke about their familial titles because Brad and Cameron are technically Seth's children's half uncles.

"I, too, have always been close to my father," Seth tells us in a phone interview. "But I've never felt responsible for Brad and Cameron the way Peggy does. I mean, I like them, and enjoy spending time with them, but I don't feel it's my responsibility to send them to college. That's probably because I have two children of my own who I have to worry about sending to college."

But, at the same time, he does not think there is anything wrong with Peggy's attitude. "Obviously, it would be nice if she met someone and had children," he says. "But at this point, I don't think her relationship to Brad and Cameron is going to change. She's always going to feel responsible for them. But that's okay. Children should have someone outside their parents they can count on."

A DEATH IN THE FAMILY

Dan was forty-one when his father, Hugh, at age sixty-eight, was diagnosed with pancreatic cancer. Father and son had never been close. "My parents got married because my mother got pregnant with me," Dan says. "It was one of those deals." They divorced when he was three, and a year later his mother married the man whom Dan would come to call his father. "My mother had two girls with my stepfather," he says. "And though they were my half sisters, I never thought of them as that. I always thought of them as my sisters."

As the years passed, Dan had what he calls "intermittent contact" with his real father, who worked in the insurance industry, first as a salesman, then as an executive. In his days as a salesman, his father moved around a lot, and every couple of years he would pass through Baltimore, where Dan grew up, and take Dan to lunch or a ball game. But that was the extent of their relationship.

Dan says, "I didn't have all that great a desire to get to know my real father because he wasn't such a wonderful guy. The truth was he was sort of a prick. And an alcoholic, too."

But toward the end of his life they spent a little more time together. In the late 1980s Dan took a teaching job in Madison, Wisconsin, not far from Chicago, where his father had settled a number of years earlier. He was living in Chicago with his third wife, Nancy, a woman in her mid forties, and their son, Andrew, who was thirteen, when the cancer was discovered.

"I'd met Andrew a couple of times before my father got sick," Dan says, "but I only really got to know him in the last month of my father's life, when I came to visit practically every weekend. By that time, my father knew he only had a short time to live, and he wanted his whole family around. I had mixed feelings about being there, because I can't say I loved the man, but my wife made me go and be with him because she said I'd regret it later if I didn't. And she was probably right."

One of the last conversations Dan had with his father was about Andrew. "My father had each one of us come into his room alone.

And he told me how much he regretted not getting to know me better, but that he was glad I was here now. And then, at the end of the conversation, he said, 'Please look out for Andrew. I know you may not see each other much, but look out for him. After all, he's your only brother.' And of course I said I would, even though in the back of my mind I was wondering whether I was really going to be able to fulfill that pledge."

Again, it was his wife who gave him the push he needed. "After the funeral, we told Andrew that he should call us if he needed anything, but my wife was the one who really made sure we maintained contact. We have two children of our own — a boy eight years old, and a girl eleven — and my wife was always saying how terrible it was that Andrew lost his father when he did. She'd say, 'Can you imagine how terrible it would be for your children to lose you in a couple of years?'"

So she was the one who kept checking in on Andrew, calling and asking how he was doing. Then she would put Dan on the phone. It started like that. And then the following summer, she invited Andrew up to Madison for a couple of weeks.

Has Dan become, then, a surrogate father?

"We aren't quite that close," Dan says. "But I could see it coming to that. For instance, he's a junior in high school now and is thinking about colleges. So I told him maybe this summer I'd take him around to some schools back East. And after I said it, I realized that was something his father would have done for him (although I don't know if my father would have). And I thought, you know, this is a very strange world we live in. Very strange."

PATTERNS

In searching for interview candidates, we encountered a host of different family combinations, including one twenty-one-year-old woman whose sixty-six-year-old father had been married three times and who had half siblings who were eighteen years older than she and sixteen years younger. From her half siblings' point of view, that made her both a second-family child as well as a first-family child. She claims she gets along well with both sets of siblings.

With some families, like Pete's and Peggy's, there was little opposition to the father's new children; but with other families, like Jane's and Vivian's, the tension between older children and father was far greater. We quickly realized what should have been obvious: a father's relationship to his older children prior to his having more children was a major factor in determining how those children felt about and related to his second set of children. If a father's relationship to his first children was strong and solid to begin with, they were more likely to remain close to him and his new family. Conversely, if the child did not get along with his or her father before the arrival of the new child, he or she was much less likely to be an active participant in the father's new family.

This seemed to hold true for most of the families we encountered, even when the opinions of the older children from the same family differed. The fact is that Pete and his older brother, John, get along well with their father's second family because they got along well with him before Katie's arrival. And while neither Jane nor Paul feel they were close to their father growing up, Jane is closer to her half sister today because her relationship with her father had improved in the years leading up to his decision to have more children.

In the case of Vivian and her brother, Brian, there is more gray area. Both were fairly close to their father growing up, and both were upset by the arrival of Ben, their half brother, but only Vivian has been able to come to terms with the situation so far. Obviously, they are different people with different personalities, but the exception here seems to be Brian's lingering anger over his parents' divorce, which also plays an important role in determining an older child's relationship to his father's second family.

SIDE A VERSUS SIDE B: A FINAL INTERVIEW

After interviewing several pairs of older siblings, we thought it would be interesting to compare two siblings' responses and play them back side by side, alternating between the siblings. We interviewed Evan and Stephanie separately on different days, with neither privy to the other's responses. Evan is a thirty-year-old banker who lives in New Jersey; his twenty-five-year-old sister Stephanie is a law student. Both Evan and Stephanie mention a third sibling, their twenty-eight-year-old sister, Linda, whom we did not interview.

EVAN: There's a twenty-year age difference between my father and his wife. My father's fifty-seven, I think. And his kids are seven and two now. They're girls. So I'm the only boy in the family.

STEPHANIE: My father's fifty-nine. His wife's thirty-eight. But he married her when she was like twenty-nine. She was one of his graduate students. He was teaching at the medical school.

EVAN: When he married Susan, my stepmother, he didn't plan on having children. That was the last thing he had on his mind. I think the agreement when he got married was not to have kids. Then she put some pressure on him and it was an issue for a while.

STEPHANIE: My brother and sister weren't affected by my father having more children as much as I was. I guess I had a hard time with his having more children because I had been the youngest before, and suddenly I wasn't the youngest.

EVAN: I have one sister who is a year and a half younger than me and one that's five years younger. The one who is five years younger had problems with my father having more children. She was just going into high school when they got married. She was the youngest. So I guess she didn't feel she was the special one any more. You know, daddy's little girl. She was always the most spoiled and favored by him. I still think it affects her having two younger sisters.

STEPHANIE: I was a senior in high school when he had the first child. None of us got told. We heard it through a relative that his wife was pregnant. And by that time, she was very pregnant. So we didn't feel part of the loop. Why didn't he tell us anything? I guess it was a combination of his being afraid to tell us and being insensitive. He doesn't have a great history of being sensitive.

EVAN: I guess it was three or four months after she got pregnant when he told me. I was surprised, but I wasn't shocked because she was so much younger and didn't have any children. In a way, I thought it was neat, but basically I thought he was nuts.

STEPHANIE: The second child he didn't want at all. In fact, I heard from an aunt that his wife had an abortion between the two kids. And later he told my older sister that he didn't want the second child. And she told us. But he didn't bring it up to either me or my brother until we were on a ski vacation and Susan was obviously pregnant.

EVAN: I know, especially after the first one, he didn't want to have any more. The second one was a war. That's why it was five years between them. And to tell you the truth, I don't think he wanted to get divorced in the first place. He's expressed that to us.

STEPHANIE: I think he's definitely changed with his second set of kids. I think he's trying to be closer to them. And not be quite as harsh with them. He has a very bad temper and he can be nasty when he wants to be. I think he's mellowed out a lot. His marriage isn't good, but I don't think he's going to get separated or divorced. He's not going to walk away from another set of kids.

EVAN: As a father, I think he's a little better with his second set of children. He's trying to atone for some of his past mistakes. He treats them differently than he treated us. He has more money now. So it's not the issue it was when we were growing up. They have a lot more things than my sisters and I had. I also think he's matured. I don't think he loses his temper as much. Growing up, I remember being in a constant war with my father, even after he left (when I was eleven) and we lived with our mother in Connecticut. These kids don't have that kind of relationship with him. He's much more patient with them.

STEPHANIE: In some sense, I've probably worked harder on having a relationship with my father than my brother and sister have. My brother and sister have frequent blowups with my father and then in between they're very civil, but they don't talk all that often. And my brother's pretty much tired of the blowups and stays away as much as possible. But I've worked at it a little more. Also, I think my father's made more of an effort with me, too, maybe because he thinks he screwed up twice with my brother and sister. I think he has a strong sense that he screwed up with his first family.

EVAN: My older sister is more like me. But I would say none of us is very close to my father. We just don't relate a lot to him. He makes an effort with us off and on. You know, I just think he's sort of overwhelmed having children in his fifties and trying to deal with a career.

STEPHANIE: Do I have a good relationship with his children? It's hard. It's definitely hard. I used to be fairly close to his wife. I don't know how much Evan told you about her. She used to be very nice and very normal. Now she's very moody, very demanding, and very hard to get along with.

EVAN: At first, I was indifferent to my stepmother. I neither liked nor disliked her. I mean, she was a nice enough person and we got along okay. But she's changed over the years. She's become a very hard person. She's sort of closed up.

STEPHANIE: Since she's had the kids, none of us have a decent relationship with her anymore, which is kind of sad. When they were first together, I would stay with them a month at a time in the summer. And I would definitely seek out some kind of mother figure. And she was there and she was always very nice. So it was strange to me that she was suddenly not so nice. Is it a reflection at all of their marriage? I'm sure that's a big part of it. They sleep in separate bedrooms now. I don't know how much they think we're aware of. But it's pretty clear.

EVAN: His marriage is his problem. I'd say that over the years, as I've drifted away from him, I've become less concerned with his problems. I try not to get wrapped up in that stuff. It only makes me frustrated since I have no say in anything he does anyway.

STEPHANIE: My stepmother has very strong feelings about what money my father should give us. That was always an issue with my parents, how much should my dad contribute? From food, to clothing, to schooling. That used to be a big issue between my parents after the divorce. Now it's a big issue between my father and his wife. If he gives me any money now for school it's very much between us. I'm not supposed to say anything to her because she would get very upset. She figures we're old enough to take care of ourselves. She wants the money for her kids. That's definitely a big source of friction. I sort of understand where she's coming from but, on the other hand, if I had kids with someone I would be psyched that he wanted to give them some money and be generous because it would show that's what he would do for my kids. But I guess she doesn't see it like that.

EVAN: Do I get along with his kids? I do, actually, which may surprise you. I really like them. I mean, I really like kids in general, so I guess that has something to do with it. But I have no problem with the kids, and to tell you the truth, in some ways — and this may sound weird — but I might not deal at all with my father if it weren't for them. I mean, part of the reason I'll go see him is so I can see them.

STEPHANIE: Last year, when I lived in New York, I saw my father's children once a month. This year, I've probably seen them four times in six months. Do I like them? Sometimes I do, sometimes I don't. It's hard, because my father feels very strongly that he wants us to be siblings. Or so he says. But that's really hard. Because I don't feel like they're my siblings at all. I definitely had a really hard time with them for a while and didn't like them at all. Now, I like them for themselves. But I don't particularly like them with their parents. They can be real terrors around their parents.

EVAN: I do think it's strange when I go out to play with them and someone will mistake me for their father. I also think it's totally bizarre that his wife is closer in age to me than to him. I think he's nuts. And so does he. He's told me that.

STEPHANIE: My father's someone who has a very limited attention span. If you're in his life right then, he's very attentive, but if you're not, he just kind of forgets. I think he gets overwhelmed with what's in front of him.

EVAN: Has he let up at all? Does he have more time? Well, I think he's as busy now as he was when we were growing up. Then he was establishing himself. Now he's established, but he still has a lot of time problems. My stepmother works full-time, too. So the kids have a full-time nanny. When we were growing up, we didn't have a nanny, but I think we had some after-school help until I became old enough to baby-sit my sisters.

STEPHANIE: His children always liked me. But they can be very hard to deal with. My father has very strong feelings about having them to do their own thing and not be too disciplined, which I don't exactly understand, because he was very disciplined with us. It's kind of bizarre, because I don't understand the lines he's drawn with them and it's something I disagree with a lot in raising kids. Sometimes they'll go absolutely wild and he lets them, and other times they'll go kind of wild and he draws a line. It's totally arbitrary.

EVAN: I think it does make him feel younger because he's around young kids and younger people. But I think if he had to choose, I don't think he would want to be in this situation at this point. I've talked to him and he's told me that he regrets doing this. I mean, he loves the kids, but this wouldn't have been his choice.

STEPHANIE: In some ways, I'm envious they have a family in that way, that they have two parents and stuff. But given the choice and looking back at my life, I'm much more happy not to have been raised with my Dad in the house. I would not have wanted to live with him full-time at all, although I do think he's a different person now than he used to be. He's getting older and looking back and regretting some of things he's done and how he's acted. I think his focus through most of his life was his work. That has been something that he's been very successful at, but it's no longer quite as rewarding. It's no longer enough. He's achieved a lot of what he wanted to achieve in his work and now he's sort of looking beyond it. I think it's sad it's taken him so long to come to that realization, and more than ever before, I feel sorry for him. I really do.

A CLEAN WAY?

Is there any "clean way" for an older father to integrate his first family with his second?

It depends on what we mean by clean. Even if a father has a good relationship with his first children, they are still going to experience moments when they wish they did not have to share his time, attention, and money with his new children. Being alone with Dad is no longer a simple proposition. Not only may he still be working (albeit shorter hours), but he now has to care for a small child or children who demand constant attention.

He also has to be sensitive to his wife's needs, which means he cannot walk out of the house whenever he wants, leaving his wife home to take care of the kids. That's a no-no, this time around. On one level, his first children think it's good that he's being more sensitive; on another, they think that it "kind of sucks" because it puts restrictions on him.

First children often blame their stepmother for those restrictions. The twenty-four-year-old son who comes home for Thanksgiving and can't go to the movies with his father like he used to wonders why his stepmother can't just stay home and watch "the kid" for a couple of hours while they're out. "After all, she was the one who wanted the child in the first place," he thinks. "If it weren't for her, he wouldn't have had more children. So why shouldn't she stay home?"

But it does not work that way. It turns out that Mother and Father are 100-percent partners. So the older son loses. His only consolation is that instead of going to the movies he can watch the football game on television. But by a cruel twist of fate, when he goes into the TV room to turn on the game, who is there but his three-year-old half sister, watching a video of *Aladdin*.

"Oh, great," his stepmother says, looking in on them. "Do you mind watching her for a minute? Your father's out back and I want to run to the store."

"No problem," he says.

As soon his stepmother leaves, he takes the remote control, zaps *Aladdin* off the screen and turns on the football game.

"Where's Aladdin?" his half sister says, puzzled. "Where's Jasmine?"

"Right there," big bro tells her, pointing to a couple of fans at the game. "The genie gave them tickets to the game. Good ones, too. Fifty-yard line."

"That's not *Aladdin*," she says, unconvinced. "I want *Aladdin*. Put on *Aladdin*."

"Aladdin was a little tired. He needed to rest for a minute. He'll be back."

If he can hold her off long enough he might get a score. Just the score, that's all he's asking for. But it's too late. She's crying already.

"I want *Aladdin*."

"One minute," he begs her. "Just one minute."

Finally, it appears. The score: 14–14. Close game. Damn, he thinks. Damn it all. But there's nothing he can do. She's screaming now, and any second his father will come into the room and give him hell. "Quit teasing her," he'll say. "The football game isn't that important."

So he changes it. He turns the VCR back on, and like magic, the tears stop, her smile returns.

"*Aladdin*," she says gleefully.

Over the years, this scene will replay itself hundreds of times in different forms. There will be petty fights over stupid things. There will be jealousy and competition. But as long as a father takes an interest in each one of his children's lives and lets them know that they are important to him, most of these incidents will fall under the category of sibling rivalry. It may not be the kind of sibling rivalry that pits children close in age against one another, but it is sibling rivalry nevertheless, and there is nothing so terrible about that.

Under these circumstances, an older father will have a relatively easy time integrating his two families. But for the older father who fails to resolve troubled relationships with his first children before having more children, there is no clean way.

"For my father, having a new wife and new children was a new beginning for him, but for me there was nothing new about it," says one first child who has yet to forgive his father for neglecting him in the past.

Another says, "You just don't get a clean slate when you have new children. That doesn't buy you anything. You have to earn a clean slate."

Ultimately, it seems, children can and will get used to almost any situation their parents push them into, but the one thing they won't accept is a parent not being there afterward to say, "See, that wasn't so bad, now, was it?" For without those words, without that assurance, the trust between parent and child is somehow lost.

7
. . . .

Eccentric Faddists or Latter-Day Columbuses?

Every Sunday, Ron gets into his 1985 BMW sedan and drives the ten minutes from his home to the train station to meet the 12:50 from New York City. He kisses his seventy-eight-year-old mother on the cheek when she steps down to the platform, and helps her into the car. As they ride together to the house, she tells him all the gossip about people he knew well as a child and remembers as they were forty years ago. They are pleasant memories — growing up on the West Side, surrounded by family and friends, at a time when kids could hang out on the city streets after school without supervision. People were always coming up to the apartment and Ron and his sister were the center of attention. "So bright," each visitor would say, taking Ron's chin between a thumb and forefinger and giving it a little tweak.

Ron's mother had been coming to "the country," as she called it, since Ron's father died five years earlier and she fell into the loneliness of an aged but still active widowhood. Since Ron's sister lived in California, it was left to him and his family to fill the void. That was not as easy as it sounded. Ron divorced in his mid forties, just after his kids left for college, ending a marriage that had hit a plateau ten years before and, despite counseling and sumptuous vacations in the Caribbean, could not survive Ron's midlife crisis. Now Ron was re-married and had a four-year-old son, Casey, born a scant thirteen months after Ron's father died. If only Marley had gotten pregnant sooner, Ron often pondered, would his father have pushed himself to live longer? Whatever the answer to that question, Ron inherited his mother, including her rent on the Riverside Drive apartment. Marley got an every-Sunday mother-in-law who still complained about Ron's ex-wife, and Casey got a grandmother who had only recently accepted Ron's second family.

"You're crazy," Ron's mother had told him when she finally noticed Marley's pregnancy. "What do you need more headaches for? Don't you already have two children? Are you going to work until you're eighty?"

Ron's mother had a way of asking the right questions, especially about finances. She was practical and knew that Ron, not his twice-divorced hippie sister somewhere out there in la-la land, would be picking up the bills for her over the next ten to fifteen years. The baby meant that she would appear as that much more of a burden for Ron and so would be that much less popular. "I only hope, for your sake, that I go fast, like your father," she would tell Ron every month or so. She also worried out loud and often about Ron's older kids, who, against her advice, had chosen not to go into engineering or medicine, two fields in which they could get good jobs. Now they were in their mid twenties, highly educated, and, in Daniel Levinson's typology, "experimenting" with different career possibilities. Ron was just thankful that they were not living at home and seemed to be able to sustain themselves. Even so, there was always the possibility that they, too, would need help.

"You're holding everybody up," Ron's mother was fond of saying. She was right. Thanks to the booming sixties, Ron had gotten a good job right away, and moved up fast. He was the first generation in his family to put away a decent amount of capital, much of it as a five-bedroom house in a classy suburb. He shared this fate with his Scarsdale neighbors, all about the same age (in their mid fifties), all atop the crest of the wave they had ridden since graduating college, all with parents who had lived far beyond anybody's expectations, and all with kids searching for secure jobs in an age of scarcity.

Ron's mother had a point about Casey, too. Having him at this stage in life was not easy. Ron would definitely not be carrying $500,000 in term life insurance if it were not for the baby. That cost $2,500 a year and went up every time Ron had a birthday. The woman who came in to sit the three days Marley worked cost another $150 a week, and that didn't include the other sitters who helped them out seven to ten hours a week. Then there was preschool. It didn't seem to make a dent back in 1970, when Ron's older kids were enrolled, but now it cost $1,700 a year just for mornings. Throw in health care and the extra clothes and toys, and they were spending about $700 to $800 a month for the pleasure of having a four-year-old.

Some of these costs, such as the baby-sitters and preschool, would eventually go down when Casey moved up to public education, but other costs would go up. Ron had thought he would retire when he was sixty-five. In the new reality, Casey would only be fourteen then. Unless he and Marley were able to put away $60,000 to 70,000 in the next few years for a college tuition nest egg, Ron might have to keep working until Casey became a freshman. He called Casey "my Porsche lease." Instead of riding around in his Porsche and hitting the clubs downtown, Ron got to exhaust himself playing with Casey and was asleep by ten-thirty at the latest.

Given the circumstances, Ron was surprised that he knew as many men his age as he did with young children. Even though they were a distinct minority, there were enough of them in his town that people rarely asked whether Casey was his grandchild. There also seemed to be more older dads than before. It made Ron wonder. They all seemed to be in the same boat, sandwiched between parents and work-age children who needed their moral and financial support, yet he and the others were willing to take on the responsibilities of a new generation. What made them do it, and what conditions had caused this upsurge in late fathering? He could not tell whether they were just eccentric faddists, frittering away the fleeting affluence of their generation on this particular form of self-indulgence, or latter-day Columbuses, sailing uncharted seas to a new world.

Ron saw arguments for both views. His generation had more money to spend than any before and probably more than his children and his grandchildren would have. His generation had also saved more, had bigger pension funds, more houses, and more leisure time. It would be easy to imagine that a generation like that would be likely to consume in all kinds of new ways, traveling more, playing more golf and tennis, and even — as a "luxury good" — having children late in life. The next generation might not be able to afford that kind of high-cost living, and it could mean a decline in the percentage of fathers over forty-five years old with young children.

But, on the other side, the worsening economic conditions for men and the much higher employment rates for women in the age of Ron's kids meant later marriage and older parenting. Divorce and new kinds of families had become a way of life during Ron's generation, a trend that was continuing among today's thirty-year-olds. If anything, Ron saw his children under greater economic and social pressures than he and his generation ever were. He could easily imagine divorce rates, marriage age, and the percentage of men avoiding marriage altogether continuing to go up as education costs rose and the restructured economy made the job environment ever tougher. Maybe more and more men and women would see families as something they did later in life, after working very hard for fifteen to twenty years. Maybe raising families would become an occupation for a later period of gradual retirement.

PERSONAL CRISIS IN HISTORICAL CONTEXT

Generations are marked by their historical experience. It has a powerful influence on their political attitudes and social behavior. The generation that reached adolescence during the Great Depression and then went to war in the 1940s had a sense of emerging as a nation from the ashes of economic catastrophe and making the world a better place for their children. They always retained the scars and pride of that era. They also tended to save a high percentage of their income, to believe in government (until it began to "fail" them in the 1970s), marry somewhat later because of economic conditions and the war, and produce large families as part of the new confidence of the postwar boom.

On the other hand, those who passed through adolescence in the 1950s, just twenty years later, had only the barest memories of the Depression. They experienced a rapidly growing affluence, a sense of their nation's world power, seemingly limitless economic opportunity, and a profound belief that social problems could be solved. They married young, parented early,[1] became socially involved, and saw their idealized image of the future shattered by political and personal events.

Earlier, we talked a lot about Gail Sheehy's *Passages* as a basis of our own understanding of what men and women go through in various stages of their lives. Sheehy based her work on Jung, Erikson, and Levinson's conception of adult development and age crises — a conception that transcends different cultures and time periods. After all, humankind everywhere has always passed through puberty, worked to feed itself, and been mortal. The puberty passage, work, and mortality frame adulthood. As Levinson writes, *"The life structure evolves through a relatively orderly sequence during the adult years.*

The essential character of the sequence is the same for *all* the men in our study and for the other men whose biographies we examined. It consists of a series of alternating stable (structure-building) periods and transitional (structure-changing) periods. These periods shape the course of adult psychological development."[2]

But books such as *Passages* (and Levinson's *Seasons of a Man's Life*) cannot escape their own historical location. Levinson brings this into his analysis by recognizing that "The self is an intrinsic part of the external world. We cannot grasp the full nature of the self without seeing how diverse aspects of the world are reflected and contained within it."[3] He and Sheehy would therefore have to admit the possibility that the seasons of people's lives could themselves be altered — both in when they occur and how — by major changes in the external world. For example, if multiple marriages and a series of different careers become the norm, the whole concept of creating a family and developing a work identity could change, both for men and for women. The nature of adult life and its crises could begin varying enormously with the greater variety of life-track possibilities.

Keep in mind that *Passages* was written in the mid 1970s. It is a document written by a member of the 1950s generation *for* that generation. *Passages* describes the coming of age, disillusionment, and hopes of a generation that, in its late thirties and early forties, faced both universal adult development issues and a particular *collective* crisis associated with that era. Despite a spell of gas lines and the beginnings of a decade of "stagflation," in the early 1970s the collective crisis was more social and political than economic. It is not surprising then that Sheehy discusses young people's ascension to adulthood in terms of seemingly limitless economic choice and describes her own mid-thirties crisis as crystallizing in the political violence in Northern Ireland (a metaphor for the larger horror of Vietnam?).

Those who came into the labor market of the 1950s and 1960s faced three-percent unemployment rates, career jobs that began at twenty-two or twenty-three, and wage increases that gave a sixth more buying power every five years. But as the teenagers of the 1950s began to turn forty in the 1970s, they saw their idealized world unravel in the social and political polarization triggered by the war in Vietnam, in racial violence, continued inequality, and white backlash. Personal lives unraveled, too. Whatever television, that increasingly powerful toy, told Americans about families, most Americans did not live "Ozzie and Harriet" lives.

Instead, they accelerated the trend to early divorce[4] — so much so that many women felt compelled to get jobs to protect themselves against a future in which they might be raising their kids by themselves. Salvation in midlife for that generation meant reconstructing a personal world that would somehow give meaning to this disillusionment.

One major advantage of the Sheehy generation is that it did not have to worry very much about jobs and incomes, at least not in the 1970s. Working-class men in the upper Midwest were crushed by the recession of 1974–75, and the nation as a whole went through a deep economic decline in the early eighties. But in general, teenagers of the 1950s built and preserved a standard in living in the 1960s and early 1970s that provided them and their children with an unusually secure lifestyle.

This economic security provided for a lot of latitude in reconstructing lives as that group passed through its midlife crisis in the 1980s, especially for the college-educated upper middle class that Sheehy addressed in *Passages*. One form of reconstruction was to marry again, probably to someone very similar — with children, with a job, with a decent income. Another was for middle-aged men, like Ron, to recover their personal ideals by using their increased economic power to create a new, ideal family.

"The first time around," Ron tells us, "I was absorbed with trying to change the world and mankind as a whole. I know that makes me sounds like a sap, but it's true. Arguably, I was trying to make the world a better place to live in for my kids, but somehow I failed to create the proper environment for them on a personal level, which I now regret."

In the 1980s, around the same time Ron was slipping into middle age, young men were still getting married and having children as Ron had done in his twenties, but the world in which they were making the transition to adulthood was different from the world of the 1950s and early 1960s, when Ron had made his transition. They still had the visions that men have in their twenties, but the visions were tempered by a new economic reality and a politics of scarcity and individual isolation. Although the economic "boom" of the mid 1980s produced fortunes for the few Michael Milkens and Donald Trumps, earning power for the vast majority of men remained stagnant, at best, and whatever gains were made were soon wiped out by the recession at the end of the decade. Meanwhile, the ideals of "fighting for democracy" and building a powerful nation in the face of Nazi and communist threats had been replaced by the ideals of individual competition in a new, highly abstract world economy where everyone was a friend and an enemy at the same time.

Young men in the 1980s were faced for the first time in this century with the prospect of having fewer material goods than their fathers. In an American society that validates men mainly on their ability to provide for their families, such a prospect made it especially difficult for these young adults to break with their parents and establish self-identity. Coming back home to live after college or making frequent calls home for money are not situations conducive to establishing oneself as an adult. Yet that is exactly what began happening in the "me" decade of the 1980s.

Levinson and Sheehy saw a man's "choice" to experiment with various work situations on the way to a final settling down after thirty as a healthy dilettantism, as long as it did not last too long. Today, for many, that is not a choice anymore, but a necessity. Young people are hired, then fired, or work "permanently temporarily." And now, with women feeling the need to establish their work careers as much as men do, the new world of work affects women's choices, too.

What will this generation of men's lives look like in the year 2010? Will it continue to produce more older fathers?

This new type of middle-aged family could be the beginning of an important social trend, but its future is counteracted by another major shift. Increasingly, a man's mid forties, which only a few years ago marked the age when he reached the apex of his career, feature a transition to lower-paying, less satisfying work — or to just plain unemployment. This means declining rather than rising average incomes at a time in life when job security and rising consumption used to be assured.

We cannot tell yet what the clash between these two trends — delayed fathering and lower income security in men's middle age — will produce. One possibility is that by the year 2010, men in their forties who either delayed children or who married early, had children, and then divorced, may find themselves still struggling to keep a job to support their older parents and/or children of previous marriages (who cannot find decent jobs, either). This financial crunch would reduce the number who decide to have children (again) in middle age.

The other possibility is that men and women who have postponed families have such a great desire for children that they are willing to ignore the rising threat to income security in late middle age. The hard choice between having a reasonable material lifestyle during a prolonged period of partial and then full retirement from work, or nurturing children while continuing to work in late middle age, could easily tilt toward the children. With changing job opportunities for men and women in middle age, later-blooming couples may also be willing to switch roles, with men staying home with the children. Twenty years from now, women in their early forties may have as good a chance or better of being the main family provider as their mid-forty-year-old husbands; that is, if husbands became more active in caring for their children.

The question, of course, is which of these trends will dominate.

Predicting social trends is a tough business. The baby boom of the 1950s and 1960s, for example, surprised most demographers. But that shouldn't keep us from trying to make projections. Our analysis assumes that the timing and size of people's families are affected by economic considerations and by a relentless desire to have a family sometime in their lives, even if that means doing it much later in life than is traditionally expected. We also assume that the economy of the industrialized world, of which the United States is an important part, is going to keep to the pattern of slower growth established in the 1980s and early 1990s, with fewer lifelong career jobs, more married women working full-time and in better jobs, and male labor force participation and earning power on a slow but steady decline. So let's begin, then, with the question of what happens to family patterns under these assumptions.

TODAY'S RISE IN MIDDLE-AGED FATHERING: A UNIQUE CASE OF SELF-INDULGENCE?

The older fathers we talked to were all products of an unusual economic period in U.S. history. They had a very different experience from those who were born in 1920 and turned twenty-nine in 1949. That would be the Depression kids, passing through adolescence in the 1930s, going to war in the early 1940s, becoming parents of the baby boomers in the late 1940s and 1950s, and retiring from the workplace in the 1980s.

In adulthood, the children of the Depression tended to have larger families (four children, on average), own their own homes, and usually their families counted on a single (man's) income. They were traditional fathers, who, as Philip Griswold tells us, came out of the

Depression experience and back from the war to a rebuilt economy in which they could be the family providers.[5] Divorce rates in the mid 1950s were relatively low, less than half of what they would rise to by the mid 1970s. In 1975, at about age 50 to 54, only 18 percent of the women of the Depression generation had divorced. Of those women born twenty years later, most of whom married in 1960s, 32 percent had divorced by their early forties.[6]

The earnings and purchasing power of men twenty-nine years old in 1949 rose steadily throughout the postwar period. Most were just high school graduates, but they still did well. If we measure everything in 1994 dollars, a young white high school graduate, twenty-five to thirty-four years old, earned a median income of $17,300 in 1949. During the next twenty years his income steadily rose, reaching a peak of $36,300 in 1969, as he reached his middle age. Meanwhile, the 10 percent of white men twenty-five to thirty-four years old in 1949 who had graduated college[7] did much better, starting at $18,500 in 1949 and hitting a peak of $58,900 in 1969.

What about Ron's group—those who turned twenty-nine in 1969 and are in their fifties today? These are the men we have been focusing on in our interviews. They, too, came into a labor market that paid them well for their work, but they were, in fact, better paid than those men who started twenty years earlier. At twenty-five to thirty-four years old, Ron's group had almost double the purchasing power that men twenty years their senior with the same level of education had at twenty-five to thirty-four. In 1969, white males twenty-five to thirty-four who had completed high school earned a median income of $31,000 (adjusted to 1994 prices), and those who completed college, more than $40,000.

They came into the job market in the Kennedy-Johnson era, just before or during the Vietnam War economic boom, and were almost all too old to serve in the war itself. The twenty-nine-year-old men in 1969 had an added advantage: They were much more likely to have finished college—more than 20 percent were graduates. This made their average incomes even higher. Their purchasing power grew less quickly in the 1970s and 1980s than earlier groups in the 1950s and 1960s had done at corresponding ages, but because the 1969 group had started at such a high level, they did as well or better at thirty-nine years old than earlier groups of men had.

By the time of their forty-ninth birthdays in 1989, though, the nation's slower economic growth had taken its toll. For the same amount of education, the men in Ron's age group were not as well off in their middle age as earlier groups had been. The saving factor was that a much greater proportion of the 1969 group had completed college, and that gave them a higher earning power even in middle age than earlier groups.

In the meantime, something else happened. The American women's movement became increasingly vocal and influential. Even though the men in Ron's group continued to earn a family wage, women wanted to be financially independent from them. Part of this drive to independence was a reaction to the postwar, middle-class family, with its undemocratic patriarchy. Another part was due to the larger movement for civil rights in the 1960s by all subordinated groups, and the rapidly increasing numbers of women going to college. And another part was due to the creeping reality of higher divorce rates in all groups during the 1960s, especially among those in their thirties who had married so young during the 1950s. The "micro" conditions of more and more women working, marrying, divorcing, and going back to work at much lower wages than men fed into "macro" conditions that legitimized and fed a powerful women's movement for equal rights.

Many men in Ron's age group supported this change, even though they were often caught up in events that they could not fully understand or adapt to. Divorce rates climbed rapidly in the 1970s, and desired family size fell from four children in the 1950s to slightly over two children in the mid 1970s. The proportion of married women with jobs rose sharply, although most worked on a part-time basis. Many divorced women had no choice; they had to work full-time and did, at very low relative incomes. As a result, single female heads of households became the largest group in poverty in the 1970s.

The 1970s also saw the beginning of another phenomenon. As family buying power was eroded by inflation in the mid 1970s, and the overall growth of men's salaries declined sharply after 1973, married women in two-parent families started coming into the job market in droves. Americans had gotten used to fast-growing family incomes based on men's wages alone. But when that stopped happening, women had to take up the slack. We can't say for sure whether this helped increase the divorce rate, but one thing is certain: It definitely put the family under more stress.

The men who turned twenty-nine in 1979, ten years after Ron

did, were teenagers in the 1960s, and entered the labor market at a much worse time. Many had gone to Vietnam or had been involved in the antiwar movement, and some had fled to Canada. Others had somehow avoided the war. Whatever they did in the late 1960s and early 1970s, their economic experience was very different from those who preceded them. Almost 30 percent of the 1979 group had finished college, and that was a plus, considering how rapidly things got bad in the 1970s for men who had only graduated high school. But incomes of young college graduates in the mid 1970s were not in terrific shape, either—they were increasing steadily, but at a very slow rate when you figure in the rapid inflation of that decade. As a result, the twenty-nine-year-olds in 1979 had less buying power than twenty-nine-year-olds in 1969, and the 1979 group did worse in the 1980s than the 1969 group did in the 1970s—for the very simple reason that the 1969 group started at a higher level and were apparently moved into good jobs that were still growing in number.[8]

But both groups, and especially Ron's, have been and continue to be affected by the business restructuring of the 1980s. Firms began cutting older workers from their core labor forces to such an extent that the real income of forty-five- to fifty-four-year-olds dropped drastically in the late 1980s and early 1990s. Mike, who just began a new family in his early fifties, tells us:

"I was one of the lucky ones who slipped through in my company's buyout because I was willing to move from Connecticut to the Northwest. Without this job and keeping my high salary and the stock options whose value went up in the last three years after my move, I would never have had the courage to have Ben and to father him at this age. The 'slip-throughs' like me are rarer and rarer. I can already see what has happened in later restructurings—they are knocking off almost everyone over forty-five years old. Ten years from now, unless things really change in companies, it will not be easy to keep a good job and benefits in middle age. I really don't see how guys like me, who are actually pretty well off, could make new families later in life."

Finally, we have the young men who entered the labor market in the 1980s and were in their late twenties and early thirties in 1989. These are today's generation of fathers, who, on the whole, are better educated than previous groups, tend to get married later (their average age of first marriage in 1989 was 26 years old versus 23.4 years old in 1979, and 22.5 years old in 1969), and their divorce rate is about the same as people ten years older.

However, a growing trend in the 1980s among white men and women was out-of-wedlock births with the father not recognizing the child. Part of the trend can be explained by incomes in this age group, which rose for college graduates in comparison to the earnings of earlier groups at twenty-nine years old, but fell for high school graduates and those with only some college. Because fewer men graduated college in the late 1970s and early 1980s than in the early 1970s, the vast majority (70 percent) of white males twenty-five to thirty-four years old in 1989 had not finished college.

The situation continued to decline in the 1990s. Thanks to the 1990–92 recession and the job shakeout in the service sector, good jobs were much harder to get in the early 1990s economic recovery than in any previous recovery. Young people are nervous, not just about getting a job, but holding one long enough to become permanent members of the middle class. And many of them feel they are not going to be as well off as their parents—people Ron's age who were the twenty-nine year-olds of 1969.

When all these numbers are put together, we can easily arrive at a pessimistic conclusion: As the men from the 1979 group hit their late forties in the middle and end of the 1990s, they may be in no state financially to have young children. The costs of raising children will continue to rise, but the income-earning prospects of middle-aged men could be in extreme jeopardy. In this pessimistic interpretation, fewer rather than more men would opt to embark on family life in late middle age.

TODAY'S OLDER FATHERING:
THE DAWN OF A MAJOR SOCIAL CHANGE?

Women's rising earnings were the other key factor affecting families in the 1980s. Although this meant that women were paid more equally to men, the good news was tempered with bad: The main reason their incomes went up was because of longer hours worked, not rising hourly wages.

During the late 1970s, at a time when men's wages were stagnating, the average working woman earned 40 percent lower wages than the average working man. But by the late 1980s, women were earning only 30 percent less—still a big difference, but a substantial shift nevertheless. By the late 1980s, there were also more families headed by women, many of whom were still in poverty, and more two-parent families who counted on women's wages than in the 1970s.

This combination of worse labor market conditions for men and better for women has changed the family. The replacement of a single, male, head-of-household wage with a family wage requiring men and women to work, has lowered fathers' capability to be the sole bread-winner. The most important demographic change this has produced is that women are older when their first child is born. By the early 1990s, a mother's age at first birth was the highest since the 1930s — twenty-four years old — up two years from the 1972 average. That in-crease may seem small, but when you take a closer look at the num-bers, you realize that the shift was actually quite dramatic, with a sharp decline in births coming from "traditional" first-time mothers (eighteen to twenty-four years old) and a sharp increase in births from higher age groups.

For women eighteen to twenty-four years old, the first-birth rate fell from about 80 per thousand in 1970 to 55 per thousand in 1991. The opposite was true for older women in this same twenty-year pe-riod: Twenty-five- to twenty-nine-year-olds had an increase from 31 to 44 per thousand, and thirty- to thirty-four year-olds and thirty-five- to thirty-nine year-olds increased even more dramatically, from 7 to 21 per thousand, and from 2 to 6 per thousand, respectively. The women's age pattern of first births in the early 1990s looked much more like the first-birth pattern in 1940, at the end of the Depression, than that of the 1950s and 1960s.

The reason for starting families later these days, however, is a lot different from what it was in the 1930s. Then, economic necessity forced young people to wait. In the 1970s, when the new pattern es-tablished itself, it was because women's education had gone way up and their job/family priorities had changed. More women wanted to establish at least some history in the labor force as capable wage earn-ers, independent of family and husband for economic support. Today, the more women earn, the longer they wait to have children (as was also true in the 1930s). Because of the continuing rise of women's ed-ucation levels and their incomes relative to men's, we would expect the trend of having first children later to continue to the end of the 1990s and beyond.

Women having children later generally means that men become fathers later, too. For at least the past thirty years, men's age at first marriage has been about two years higher than women's. (They be-come first-time fathers about two years older, too.) So the trend for an increasing fraction of women to have first children in their thirties means that there are correspondingly more higher-educated fathers who do not father before they turn thirty-five years old, and a much greater number who have their second child when they are in their forties.[9]

Unless something strange happens — such as a major war or a drastic change in our environment or the discovery of a new, untransportable technology that gives the U.S. economy the ability to produce goods cheaper and better than in Asia — the trend toward higher and higher education, more women working full-time and for steadily higher wages compared to men, and toward smaller families and high divorce rates, is likely to continue well into the twenty-first century. Economic factors will most likely prolong the trend of later marriages and first-time births, which in turn should lead to a growing population of fathers over forty-five years old with young children.

But there is also an economic countercurrent. It is becoming more expensive to have children, and things are getting financially more difficult for older men, even for those who are well educated. This means that fathering in middle age will require greater sacrifices in the future.

Karl Day, a fifty-seven-year-old with a three-year-old son, told *USA Today*, "My little boy will start college when I turn 72. Retirement is one of those planning horizons I don't have to worry about anymore."[10]

And Jerrold Lee Shapiro, a psychologist, tells us, "I think a lot about how having kids now means I can't retire. It's a real choice. I'm fifty-one and I've got a six-year-old. I wanted to be a full-time writer when I reached fifty-two. It's painful to deal with all the stuff at universities these days, but I can't afford to leave now. I'm hoping to at fifty-five, but it's unlikely. All that depends on how much my wife will work. It all means that there is a double loss here: one is a loss in terms of what I want to do with this part of my life; the other is a loss in terms of my children, particularly with my young son."

Yet even with these problems, the data and our interviews suggest that people's drive to have children is great, and they find ways to raise families even when times are difficult. Among many ethnic groups where extended families are still the rule, having large families is in part also motivated by the search for security in old age. Even with young people having a harder time finding good jobs, this motivation may creep back into the white middle class if old-age security becomes a serious problem again. The more children, the greater the possibility that one of them will help their parents in hard times. Such demographics make a strong case for continued increases in older fathering, maybe back to rates prevalent in 1940, even if for different reasons.

A shift to older fathering makes sense in another way. Despite rising average education, younger men's incomes corrected for inflation have fallen steadily since the early 1970s, after rising rapidly since 1940. The incomes men earn still go up as we acquire work experience, especially if we have a college education. But on average they rise a lot less than in the past, and the rise tails off sooner—in our mid forties rather than in our early fifties—than it did for men who hit middle age in the late 1960s and late 1970s. So it makes sense—again, especially if we have a college education and professional careers—to wait at least until we get into that higher income level of our thirties to have children. It also makes sense that our wives work full-time longer and establish careers to help carry the family through our much more insecure, lower income as men hit middle age. Add in a likely divorce in our thirties, and having children may be postponed even longer.

The way we *behave* as older fathers has changed along with the demographics. In the old days, dads just provided for the children. We did not actively *care* for them. As James Levine, who has long been head of the Fatherhood Project of the Families and Work Institute in New York City says, "We're legitimizing the idea of men as caregivers. There's still a stigma attached, but the message is getting out that it's okay."[11] The message is being delivered home by the gradual demise of the long-term, single-job career, and a new wage system that requires mother and father to be flexible in finding ways to maximize income. If families are going to provide decent environments for children under current work conditions, this flexibility is going to have to include fathers who are good at nurturing and childcaring—not exactly skills that men have historically been encouraged to master.

Jerrold Lee Shapiro, who has long been concerned with issues of fathering, writes:

> For modern men in Western cultures, becoming a father is a biological, social, and emotional process. It is, however, one for which there is little consistent training, norms, or guidelines. Most men learn very early that the predominant role of fathering is to be the *financial provider* for the family. They also learn, in a variety of ways, that fathering is somehow secondary to mothering."[12]

THE SANDWICH EFFECT

Ron's group — the men who have reached middle age in the 1990s — is not unique in having to care for both young and old. Extended families have always operated that way. The difference in the 1990s is that the age at which the squeeze takes place is being extended into men's fifties. Not only are their parents living longer, but their kids are taking longer than before to find secure employment. The causes of these two phenomena are not likely to go away. If anything, the world economy will become even more competitive. Giants such as China and India, with their masses of low-cost laborers, are poised in the next twenty-five years to be major players. In America, young people and middle-aged men may have even harder times getting and holding on to jobs with decent pay. And if anything, longevity is on the rise. Parents are going to live longer.

It seems, then, that everything is happening later, except that at the same time, everything is less secure. The men who turn fifty in 2010 will, on average, have younger children — many of them with early teenagers or younger still living at home — than their parents (Ron's sixties generation). Their fairly well-off parents will still be living, probably well into their eighties. For all the high incomes they earned back in the 1960s, 1970s, and 1980s, many will have run through most of that money by 2010, or it may not have been enough in the first place to take care of astronomical nursing and home care costs (still not covered by universal health care) in 2010.

The choices of the middle-age transition could look a lot different fifteen years from now. The fifty-year-old men of 2010 will have much less purchasing power than their parents to handle this combination of responsibilities. The cost of college for their children plus the home care costs could make for one long middle-age nightmare, hardly the stuff of the American dream.

At the same time, middle-aged women will be much more responsible for holding families together financially than they are even today. Traditionally, men were supposed to protect their families from physical and fiscal harm, and if you were to ask fathers today what they believe their primary responsibility is, they would probably give you that answer. But the labor market could prevent men from carrying out this responsibility alone, or could force them to give up having a family or to share both financial and childcare responsibilities with their spouses. Longer-living parents (with fewer children) may be as much the cause of this change as having children later in life. Yet, whatever the cause, the midlife options will surely change considerably for the generation that is now turning thirty.

WHICH DYNAMIC WILL PREVAIL?

Current social and economic trends are forcing a growing number of college-educated young people to delay not only marriage, but, to an even greater degree, children, with the fastest rising first-child birth rates among women and men in the group that is older than thirty years old, which doesn't even account for the growing number of adoptions among couples in this category.

But there is a catch. From a financial standpoint, it is getting more and more stressful to have young children during the middle-age transition and beyond. Many families, as we have seen, are willing to take on that obligation, no matter what the cost. In middle age, young children can be a wonderful treat — a source of new meaning in a world whose other qualities are wearing thin. In many cases, a new child at this age is a reaction to the materialist quest. One result of early "obsolescence" for working men may be to switch them over to a simpler, gentler way of life, working for less money and enjoying family life more. The middle-aged family may work to model a new set of relationships.

8

. . . .

Is Late Fathering Bad for Kids?

"My relationship with my three-year-old, Annie, is so close that I really worry about something happening to me," a real estate broker, Hal, tells us. "At fifty-seven, I have friends my age and just slightly older already getting heart problems and cancer. There is nothing I can do about it, but it concerns me. I admit it—it's on my mind. So I end up trying to protect her by putting as much money as I can in a trust. It's a way of making myself feel better, but it doesn't solve the problem."

"It blows my mind that my brother is thirty and has a dad," says ten-year-old Miles, referring to his fifty-five-year-old father's oldest son from a former marriage. Then, somewhat wistfully, he adds, "I don't think I'll have the experience of having my father around when I'm thirty."

When we hear Hal and Miles voice their inner fears, it is understandable that our society is uncomfortable with older parenting. Like most people in the world, we in the U.S. are very aware of doing things at the "proper time" in life, and our institutions help condition us to think this way. Try to get a particular job at forty-five when employers have defined it as work for thirty-year-olds. No matter how qualified you are and how modest your salary demands, there is almost no chance of getting the job. The same goes for first marriages. A man or woman who waits until forty to marry is psychologically suspect.

So when couples have children in middle age, most of us think they are out of sync. Their behavior is not "as it should be." We tend to believe that older parents have serious drawbacks. We know that they are more likely to get sick and die when their children are in their teens or even younger. They also seem too old to roughhouse with their kids, and we generally stereotype them as having a grandparent mentality that spoils and overprotects children. Most of us regard these characteristics as having harmful effects on children, and it does not take much of a moral leap to suggest that older parenting is socially irresponsible.

In his book *Latecomers, New York Times* journalist Andrew Yarrow had this to say about children of older parents who lost their parents early:

> These children had to deal with powerful and complex feelings of grief and helplessness, which are difficult at any age. In addition, bereavement in childhood often is linked to adolescent and adult emotional distress. The immediate and short-term effects of loss can include feelings of betrayal, anger, and vulnerability and can result in difficulty making emotional attachments as well as insomnia and hyperactivity.[1]

Society also frowns on other aspects of older parenting. Until recently women have been limited by biology on the age that they can give birth (although even in-vitro technology, with its exorbitant costs and complicated feelings associated with carrying another woman's egg, has its constraints). But men can become fathers at almost any age. A surprising number of men, married to much younger women, become fathers well after sixty. Yet people tend to disapprove of these marriages and the resulting families. They seem to have have a mercenary character—the aged "gentleman" parading his young "acquisition" on his arm, while the young acquisition glances over his shoulder at his bank account. Our cynicism spills over into pity for the children, who, while they may end up with trust funds, have to pay for them with a sick or dead father or, worse, an ugly divorce and uncaring stepmothers and stepfathers. We gleefully consume autobiographies by Hollywood children to get the grim details of these scenarios.

But are we right to jump to these conclusions? Is older fathering really a bad deal for the children, even considering the greater risk of an earlier sickness or death?

Older fathers and mothers themselves are not a particularly good source for assessing the advantages and disadvantages of middle-aged parenting. They have a vested interest in feeling good about what they are doing. Even so, many of the fathers (and mothers) we interviewed admitted to serious concerns about the effect their age had on their kids. We also found that the moral dilemma for older fathers who are having children so late in life is often muddled by their desire to preserve relationships with younger women, and that it is these younger women, not the men, who are the driving force behind the decision to procreate.

The children of middle-aged fathers are more likely to be honest about the negative effect of having an older parent (or parents), although the moral implications of their message is not clear even to them. These children as a source present another set of problems. There are so many possible factors, both positive and negative, involved in their evaluation that you almost have to know the specific circumstances under which they "came late."

OLDER FATHERS AND THE MORTALITY PROBLEM

Ask an older father about his young child's chances of having a father in adulthood, and you get a predictable answer: "I can't do much about it but be there for him now," or, "I think I'm going to live a long time — there's longevity in my family — anyway, I'll do my best." Some of these fathers did agonize over the decision to have a child so late in life, and the risk of leaving the scene prematurely was and is an important part of their concern as their children grow up. For many, it was a tough decision to go ahead and have or adopt a child when they might not be around for more than ten or fifteen years. But few middle-aged men (even those without young children) believe that the mortality issue is critical in choosing whether or not to have a late family.

This makes sense. Unless the baby is the man's first, middle-aged men are not usually the ones who initiate the move to parent. They may give in joyfully, or resist only to cave in eventually, but their main motivation is preserving a relationship they need and want, or simply honoring the desire of their younger spouses to nurture a child.

On the other hand, when childless men marry late, they have a lot to do with the fathering choice. Most very much want to have children. One such man is Richard Griffin (his real name), who lives on a shady street in Cambridge, Massachusetts, near Harvard University, with his wife and twelve-year-old daughter, Emily. He is a charming, friendly man in his late middle age, full of spiritual energy. He is also a contemplator, someone who, by his own admission, thinks things over and is definitely not prone to making compulsive decisions. Whether this is unusual or not for a man is debatable, but Richard himself *is* unusual. For more than twenty-five years he was a Jesuit priest, immersed in a "sacred world" until he left the order at age forty-seven, in 1975, and married a year later.

Richard has written about his passage into middle age and out of formal religious life in an essay, "From Sacred to Secular: Memoir of a Mid-Life Transition Toward Spiritual Freedom."[2] His is a story of commitment and faith. In his youth, he had a profound belief that he would find the meaning of life through the discipline and inner prayer prescribed by the Jesuit order, but as the years passed, he gradually came to the realization that the deepest meaning of life was in progress away from the rigid structure of organized religion and toward freedom. "If I never did anything else," he wrote, ". . . having laid hold of personal freedom would give my life significance."[3]

If anyone would be focused on the moral implications of his turn to fatherhood in late middle age, it would be Richard Griffin. Even after leaving the Jesuits, he remained deeply religious and attached to the Catholic church. His wife shared these values with him, and when she became pregnant at forty, four years after they got married, they decided not to use amniocentesis, but instead to "proceed in hope and accept whatever God gave us. Our reverence for the life of our child even before birth would have prevented us from violating it, in any event."

The child was born perfectly healthy. Richard would later write, "This reality made me feel truly blessed by God. No matter what else happened I had been given the altogether precious gift of a child and at an age when I did not expect it." Richard and his wife experienced the birth of their daughter as "an ecstatic event," producing "intense euphoria"—a religious experience very different from what Richard had found in his youth, but a religious experience nonetheless.

Someone who found the birth of his first child at fifty-two years old a consecration of his search for freedom might be expected to also weigh this freedom against the child's own choices and experiences. Richard did. He had reservations: What would it be like for her to have such old parents and what would happen to her if something happened to him? Yet in the end, he came out believing that the life he helped create was not only a blessing but was blessed.

"Being a father of a young child did not carry with it any social problems," he wrote. "In fact, people expressed nothing but pleasure at my good fortune. Nor has it carried perceptible disadvantages for my daughter herself. Contrary to imaginings of some media types, older parenthood does not result in handicaps for children. I even argue the opposite: having parents middle aged assures offspring of greater stability than other children may have."

Interviewed on Boston TV, Richard sounded this same theme. Although the news story began with a shot of Richard and Emily playing catch, he told the interviewer that he could not do all the things with Emily that a younger man could do. However, he did not see this as a major handicap. "Sometimes, deep down in me, I've had concerns, but I'm not fixated on them," he said. "One of my goals in life is to live long enough so that she is established as a young woman."

Richard and Emily's relationship is surely different from what it might have been had she been born when he was thirty. But that baby would not have been Emily, and much of what she is — a thoughtful twelve-year-old with a wide range of interests — is due to having been born to the parents she had when she was.

Richard's spiritual encounter with his child is not atypical of late first-time fatherhood, even for people who are not as committed to a particular body of religious belief. But most middle-aged fathers defend the morality of their decision in more practical terms: They usually choose fatherhood to preserve a relationship with a younger woman. She wants to have a child, then so does he. In effect, she makes a decision that he must agree to go along with or find someone else. So the morality of late fatherhood is wrapped up with women and men who fall in love and the natural and inevitable desire that produces — especially for women without children — to consummate their love with a baby.

Men do not have to be great philosophers to justify late fatherhood under such circumstances, even if they worry about how long they might or might not be around to father, and how an early exit or a protracted illness might affect their child. They see their willingness to father as fulfilling the needs of another human being. From their point of view, if they are good providers and nurturing fathers for as long as they can be, their death has only small moral consequence. In fathering a child for the woman he loves and loving and caring for that child, our middle-aged father sees himself as just and good.

And why not? We may not like the idea that older men seek out younger women, or that younger women marry older men, but a certain number do (although the average age difference in couples where the father is older than forty-five is less than ten years). Should the woman in such a relationship deny herself a child because her partner has a shorter remaining life span than younger men, or is more likely to become seriously ill before the child is fully grown? We doubt many women would accept that moral position. Most men would probably be more willing to opt out of relationships (or never enter them) with younger women rather than have a child they could not nurture and provide for properly.

Go back to Henry, the recently married medical researcher with the six-month-old baby boy. This is exactly the situation in which he found himself. "Look," he says, "you have to decide. When she's thirty-seven and you're fifty, you're a fool if you think you are going to keep her and deny her a child. Even if you get away with it, that decision will transform the way she sees you. It's not exactly as if you had had an affair, but it has a similar impact. You have closed down her potential space, her vision of herself, and bitterness will set in. I would say that it is much more of a sin to use the power of your love to do that than to bring a child into a family where dad might die fifteen years later.

"Besides, I think that my kid is pretty lucky to have been born to middle-aged me. He is going to have a lot of my time, will get to travel, will live in a nice house, and have a stable family with parents who know who they are. I wish I had grown up in that atmosphere."

But would he have been as hard-driving and successful if he had the same things his son now has growing up?

"Maybe it would have taken my hard edge off earlier," he says. "Anyway, it doesn't matter. He's going to be a product of his environment just like I was. I think it'll be a lot better for him than for me, so I feel good about what I've done. And I have no intention of departing early. Earlier in this century, fathers regularly had children at thirty and died at fifty or fifty-five. I had a son at fifty-two and have a very high probability of living until my late seventies or later. It's about the same risk, with the same moral implications. The only difference is that society is still stuck on images of certain ages as if nutrition and medicine had not changed in seventy-five years."

Michael is a philosopher and mathematician, teaching at a university in the Northwest. He is seventy-two, with a fourteen-year-old daughter and a five-year-old son, so he is not in a position to use Henry's argument about having plenty of years left for his son. Instead, he tries to balance the good against the bad. Michael's attitude about the world is that there are no simple answers to anything that involve complex decisions. "I am very skeptical of simple arguments about the permanent harm caused children by a father's or mother's death," he says. "I am much more sympathetic to understanding the effect of parents' age on the child in terms of what relations are in the family—what works and what doesn't—and the psychological character of the people involved, parents and kids. In other words, for me something like age is much less significant than the psychological makeup of the individuals involved. My mother died when I was only four and a half, and it was a bad thing—I remember being angry—but it's impossible to assess if there were any long-term damage to me. It very much depends on what your perception is of the course of my life's events. Anyway, my father remarried and I had a very good stepmother to grow up with.

For Michael, the bottom line was that people's decisions to have children could not be based on actuarial tables. In his case, since he didn't have to worry about the cost, the chief argument he had with himself was whether it would be rewarding to have children so late in life, and the answer was a resounding yes.

"I may have a strange conception of morality," he says. "This issue of older parenting and the possible death of a parent has got to be something of a second- or third-order moral question. When you compare it to all the other things like the violation of individual rights and crime, it's just not that important. Even in the case of families, what is the cost for a child whose parents are in their twenties and get a divorce when he is fourteen? Is that worse than a death? My own personal view is that divorce at fourteen is worse."

Michael's wife is thirty-two years younger than he is. His son was born when she was thirty-six, which, if you do the math, made Michael sixty-eight. "If we were going to have a second child, it was the moment of decision," Michael says. "She was nearing the end of her fertility and I was—well, I was getting pretty old. So, in that sense, my age—just as much as my wife's—was actually a catalyst in having this second child."

We talked to many couples where the threat of a man's death was actually the catalyst for having a child. Is this immoral? Unfair to the child? It depends how you look at it. Should women of any age avoid having children with their husbands because their relationships may end in sickness, death, or divorce? If we really believed that, young women with young husbands would be even less likely to feel morally secure about childbearing, since such a high percentage of marriages among those in their twenties ends in divorce.

LOVE AND DEATH

Donna works for a school district in Georgia. She met Marcel when she was a graduate student at the university where he taught economics. He was forty, divorced, and sharing the custody of his two children. Donna and Marcel fell in love, and, despite her family's and friends' strong opposition, she moved in with him and his kids. Ten years later, much to everyone's surprise, they were still together. By that time, his son had gone away to college and his daughter, Helene, who was seventeen, was living with Donna and Marcel full-time. Over the years, Donna and Helene had developed a close relationship, fostered partially by Donna's youth. The two young women, separated by only sixteen years, told each other sister secrets and whispered to each other at parties. Marcel could sometimes see them giggling in corners, which made him happy and bound him closer to Donna, even though they were not married.

Then one night, without warning, Marcel suffered a major heart attack. He was only fifty, and in great physical condition, but there he was being rushed in an ambulance to the hospital, where he was put on life-support systems. The news only got worse. The doctors told Donna that Marcel had no hope to survive. His heart was simply too damaged. The only question was what to do with his other organs. They were in good condition and were candidates for transplantation, but since Donna was not legally Marcel's wife, she felt that she could not make such a decision alone—even with Helene. So she called Marcel's ex-wife, who lived in Florida.

"I'm sorry," she said to the ex-wife over the phone. "But I didn't know whom to turn to. At least you were married to him and are the mother of his children. I think you have as much a right to make this decision as I do."

"I'll be up on the next flight," the ex-wife said.

While she waited for Marcel's ex-wife to arrive, Donna went home to get some sleep. Helene stayed at the hospital to keep watch over Marcel, who the doctors said would die as soon as the life-support system was removed. Donna searched for something to do, someone to talk to. In the end, she decided to call a young doctor friend who knew Marcel well. She wanted him to go check on Marcel so he could advise her on the organ decision.

Of course he would go, the doctor said, and rushed down to the hospital to pay a last visit to his friend. But when he got to Marcel's room, what he found there shocked him. Marcel was sitting up in bed, the life-support tubes dangling from his body and head. He looked totally confused but quite alive.

"Where am I?" Marcel said to his friend. "What's going on?"

"You're in a hospital," his friend said. "And from what people have been telling me, you've been dead for six hours."

In the months following Marcel's surprising recovery, Donna did a lot of thinking. She realized that he might be around for ten or twenty years, but that it could be ten or twenty months. They had lived together for more than a decade, and she loved him very much. Had he died, she would have had nothing from their relationship—nothing that represented their deep commitment. She could not forget the emptiness she had felt the night the doctors told her he had no hope for survival.

Marcel had never wanted to have more children, and now, especially, would not consider fathering a child. His chances of being around for any significant length of time were slim—very slim. But Donna took matters into her own hands. She stopped using her diaphragm, and within three months she was pregnant. She didn't tell Marcel, though. He figured it out on his own, and when he did, he was not happy at all. But Donna held firm. She wanted to have a child with him at any cost, even it meant jeopardizing their relationship. That, however, did not happen. As she grew larger, he grew more accepting of her pregnancy, and when it became clear that she was going to have twins, he became alternately fascinated with the idea and depressed by it. My God, he thought, life with twins!

When we met Donna and Marcel, Helene was already in college and the twins—a boy and a girl—were three years old. In the three years since the twins were born, Marcel had reorganized his life to spend more time at home and rest. He complained to us that the children were "wearing him out." But when he said this, there was a glint in his eye that proceeded to brighten the more he talked about his "babies."

Donna watched him as he spoke, then would steal an occasional look at us and give a quick smile. She knew she had done the right thing. The twins were part of their life together and gave it a dimension that transcended them as individuals. If they lost their father when they were young—an everyday possibility, even though Marcel followed a strict diet and an exercise program—they would always have her and, through her, she reasoned, vivid memories of him.

Cut to Washington, D.C. The year is 1988, and Harry, in his mid fifties, is living with his second wife, Ellen, who is forty. This is not only a second marriage for him, but for her, too. He has three grown children and a grandchild, with a second on the way. Neither Harry nor Ellen wants children — at least, that's what they say to each other — and besides, Ellen thinks that she's too old to conceive.

One month, she misses her period. Then another goes by, and she misses it again. "Am I starting to hit menopause?" she asks Harry. Harry is not sure. Just to check, they buy a pregnancy test kit.

The next thing they know, they are staring at a stick and watching it turn blue. They cannot believe it. They do the test again, and the same thing happens. They look at each other. Harry is in shock, but gradually, and with increasing speed, he begins to realize that Ellen is brimming with joy.

"I didn't dare say anything because of the way I felt," Harry tells us almost six years later. "She was radiant, but I just couldn't react the way she wanted me to. I couldn't feel what she wanted me to feel."

Two weeks after the pregnancy test, her gynecologist verifies that Ellen is almost three months pregnant. Harry wants Ellen to be happy, but cannot imagine raising a baby again. He knows all too well what it means. Even as his children went through their twenties, living in distant cities, he had had to provide a lot of moral support. It went on and on. Starting at his age, he probably won't be there for this child in its twenties.

Later that week, almost forgotten in the turmoil of the pregnancy, Harry has an appointment with the ophthalmologist. His right eye has been bothering him for months, but he ignored it until Ellen made him set up the appointment. It doesn't take long for the doctor to figure out the problem. Harry has a small tumor in his eye, which turns out to be malignant.

"Suddenly, everything was different," explains Harry today. "One minute, I'm worried that I won't last thirty years, so I shouldn't have a child; the next minute, Ellen's pregnancy is the greatest thing that could have happened — a child that would remain behind for her when I was gone. All I could think was that God had superimposed the two pieces of news to help us pass through whatever was going to happen. Instead of being depressed, I was philosophical. No matter how things ended for me, my relationship with Ellen would be immortalized in this baby growing inside her. I don't know how I would have handled the prospect of an untimely death without that untimely pregnancy."

Harry's operation was a success. Last year, he celebrated his sixtieth birthday, cancer free. His and Ellen's daughter, Raquel, is five, two years younger than Harry's granddaughter. Does he feel guilty about not wanting Raquel until he needed her? Hardly. Refathering has been too passionate an experience for him to carry that baggage. And Harry knows that he would never have tried to prevent Ellen from having their child, tumor or no tumor. She would not have given in, anyway, so what choice did he have? Walk out of the marriage?

"Does a man who loves his wife leave her because she wants his child?" Harry asks. "When did that ever happen?"

THE VIEW FROM THE CHILDREN'S ROOM

What do the children of middle-aged fathers feel about their older parent? When they become adults do they look back at their childhood with anger? Do they see their middle-aged father (or parents) as having done them harm?

The one large study dealing with this subject shows that the memories are highly varied. In *Latecomers*, many of the children Andrew Yarrow heard from resented the age of their parents, but were much more likely to harbor ill feelings about their childhood when they were the last in a line of five or six, the "tail-enders" or "accidents" — the children of parents who started having offspring in their twenties and continued into their forties.

"Such veteran parents were often remembered as having little emotional and physical energy to devote to their last child," Yarrow wrote. "Although they were frequently seen as having more experience raising children, they were sometimes perceived as worn out by two decades of child-rearing and, as a result, less attentive to the needs and wants of their youngest child."[4]

A child of disengaged parents, growing up surrounded by the "knees" of older siblings, usually does not need to imagine the attention and care that his or her predecessors received. It is ever present in the relationship the parents continue to have with them. "Being the last born of seven children, I got little attention," one of Yarrow's respondents reported. "As I grew older, it got worse. My older brothers and sisters were having kids of their own and would call on mom and dad for assistance. So, they became less concerned with me and what I wanted. They were definitely tired of raising their own kids."[5]

Logically, the child (and later, the adult) blames the parents' age for the distance he or she feels from them. Age symbolizes the unfortunate chronological order, the tiredness, the "accident," and the burden of the anachronistic child. Another of Yarrow's respondents said, "My parents had been parenting for twenty years when I came along, and I feel I missed out on their best years. They had lost interest in the events of my life. If it had been the first time around, maybe it would have been more appealing to them."[6]

But some older parents end up paying a lot of attention to the "baby" of the family, in which case the age resentment factor seems to go down. Those latecomers appreciate the parents' experience, their willingness to trust and give them responsibility — to "lengthen the leash," as many of them put it.

In any case, these are the waning wave of latecomers. Although many such children are still being born, the most rapidly growing group of children of middle-aged parents are the ones who are "planned" and very wanted. They are Yarrow's "onlies"—the one or two children of couples who postponed parenthood while they majored in career enhancement and workaholism, then focused on family life with just as much energy and devotion as they had given to work.

Yarrow wrote, "In some respects, what is learned from the lives of only children of older parents suggests what the experiences of present and future generations of latecomers are likely to be. Since later-born children will increasingly be members of small families, they may have more-involved, adoring parents but may still feel lonely because of their small families and worried about having to care single-handedly for aging parents."

Yarrow's letters from the "onlies" of middle-aged parents have a different tone than those from last children in large families. These only children received the benefits of being very wanted, including lots of time, affection, and encouragement from their parents. They also generally benefited from their older parents' well-off financial status and the close bonding of small family units. The most common complaint among later-born onlies was that they felt more set apart from their peers than only children of younger parents. They also tended to blame their being only children on their parents' age.[7]

The most surprising results come from the responses of children of much older fathers, over fifty years old when the child was born. Yarrow wrote:

[T]hose born when their fathers were fifty or older consistently had more positive recollections [when compared to responses of those whose fathers were thirty-five to forty-nine years old]. These feelings were particularly strong concerning their fathers' impact on their personalities, maturity, and social skills. . . . Children of fifty-plus fathers much more often said that their fathers were helpful to them and that their relationships were closer during childhood and adolescence than did children of the younger fathers. A greater proportion also saw their fathers as role models and denied that there was a generation gap.[8]

MY FATHER DIED

Carol Weston, a writer living in Los Angeles, had an intense, secure, fun relationship with her father, William Weston, who was forty-three years old and an accomplished documentary filmmaker and television producer when Carol was born. But when Carol was just twenty-five, he died, leaving her heartbroken. "I was the apple of my father's eye. When your father dies, you ask yourself, am I still an apple? For the rest of my life, I don't have a father here, to play with my kids, to read my books."[9]

Ann is the fifth of five children, born when her father was fifty-two and her mother forty. She was an accident or, in her words, a "change of life child." According to the family story, her father wanted her, but her mother only agreed to the pregnancy if Ann's father would hire someone to take on responsibility for their store.

"My mother wanted my father to ease up at work and spend more time at home," she tells us. "So he did, and I was allowed to be born." The result was that Ann and her next older sister, four years her senior, had a very close relationship with their father, much closer than that of their older siblings, who were twenty, eighteen, and sixteen when Ann was born.

"I spent a lot of time with my dad," she continues, "and we had a great time. He spoiled me and my sister, but he also gave us a lot of responsibility for our behavior. We were expected to act older and wiser than the other kids our age. It made me more confident of myself— that I could make decisions — so I acted more adult even when I was a teenager."

When Ann was twelve, her father suffered a serious stroke. The family sold the store and moved to Los Angeles to be nearer Ann's older siblings and their families. But the brunt of taking care of her father fell to Ann, her mother, and her sister. "It was hard," she says. "My father was partially paralyzed, and I had to spend a lot of time at home helping my mother, just at an age when I felt like being with my friends. I got even closer to my dad, but I definitely resented him. I felt tied down, and it was his fault. He was too old when I was born, but then I owed my existence to him. These were heavy contradictions for a twelve-year-old. When he died three years later, I was relieved. I missed him, but at least he was released—and so was I. Now I look back and I can honestly say that I had a wonderful father and that I was very close to him. I do not mind now, in my early twenties, that he was an older father and that he is not around. I know that I got so close to him because he was at a stage in life when he could spend so much time with me. But I certainly was angry with him when he was sick—I can't deny it."

Lana was adopted a few days after she was born by an interracial couple—her adoptive mother was white and her adoptive father black. She was well matched, because her birth mother was also white and her father black. The adoption was closed, so Lana did not know any more about her birth parents than their race until she was in her twenties and began the long search for them. Her adoptive parents had two natural children—both boys—and badly wanted a girl. Lana fulfilled that dream. Her adoptive father was forty-two when she was born, and her mother forty.

"I was adopted into an interracial, middle-class family with two sons," she says. "It was in the late 1960s. My earliest memories of my father are of his coming home from work to our house in an integrated suburb of Minneapolis. My dad worked for a film distribution company, and he traveled a lot. So I remember him on weekends. He would be the person in charge of barbecuing. 'Dad's home!' I remembering everyone shouting. He would always pick me up first thing when he got home. I was daddy's little girl, and he always treated me as someone very special—a little spoiled, really. On Father's Day, when I was five years old, he brought me a portable record player. I'll never forget that—he bought me a present on Father's Day."

As Lana retrieves images of her father from the distant past we notice that her voice is tinged with both happiness and sadness; clearly, she has fond memories of him, but at the same time, she seems sad there are so few of them.

"When I was six years old we moved to California," she goes on. "My dad had a business opportunity. He left his job and left his insurance, and he was almost immediately diagnosed with lung cancer, and he had no insurance—it was a huge change in our lives. He was at home until the two months of his life when he was flown out to the Mayo Clinic, nearer our family back in Minnesota. He died in July when I was eight years old. The hardest thing for me was that I never got to say good-bye to him. I'm really sorry about that. We celebrated his fiftieth birthday in the clinic, and he was trying to be jovial and vivacious—that's what he had been like when he was well—but his spirit was was gone at the end. That's the last time I saw him. He died a few days later, and some relatives came over to where I was staying and shook my hand. `Your dad died,' they told me, like in a formal announcement."

Lana's older brother became her role model, and he was a great help to her as she grew up. But once her dad died, the family moved from an integrated neighborhood, where there was an element of biculturalism, into the white suburbs of southern California, where it was a lot harder for Lana and her brothers. People were always trying to test them, trying to figure out "who and what they were." Lana had an especially terrible time in junior high. The black kids teased her because she was white, and the white kids treated her badly because she was black. Through it all, she believed things would have been different if her father had lived. Not only would they have lived in a "better, more accepting" neighborhood, but they wouldn't have had to struggle so hard financially.

"Although in my adulthood I haven't had the greatest relationship with my mom," Lana says, "she has helped me a lot by projecting a very positive image of my father. When my mom is in a context where she feels that she can talk about it, hearing the funny and embarrassing stories going to back to Minneapolis, helps make my father into a three-dimensional, real person. He still remains largely mythological, and I long to make him more real in my own mind."

In her early twenties, Lana began searching for her birth mother, whom she found but has not yet met. And now she is searching for her birth father, who may not even know she exists.

"So you could say that I'm on a constant search for parents," she says. "For a more complete image of my adoptive father, who died when I was eight, and for the identity of my birth parents. It's not easy for my poor mother. She feels that I am somehow unsatisfied with her. The fact that she is now in her sixties makes it all even more threatening. She is worried that I will connect spiritually with my younger birth mother in some way that I cannot with her. I don't see it that way at all. I just need *more* connections, not substitutes."

"SOMETIMES WHEN I'M LYING
IN BED AT NIGHT . . ."

Children with older parents seem to worry more about them dying than do children with normal-aged parents, and with good reason. The probability of a thirty-year-old father living to sixty, when his just-born child would be thirty, is 85 percent. The probability of thirty years' additional life for a forty-year-old man is 68 percent, and for a fifty-year-old, 41 percent.[10] So, on average, the children of late middle-aged fathers have a much lower chance of having a dad around to see them marry or play with the grandkids. We can imagine that men who marry younger women and have children in their forties and fifties are more active, in better shape, and live longer, but they still have many fewer years left when their children are born than do younger fathers. And their kids think about these things. They are acutely aware of their parents' age, and of how their friends view their older parents.

Awareness does not mean condemnation or even negative feelings. The preteens we talked to all had fathers in their late fifties or early sixties. They all thought of their fathers as unusual in that they were much older, but all had highly positive things to say about the attention they received, their fathers' appearance and attitude toward life, and their relationships with them. All these children saw themselves as very fortunate, on the whole, to have the fathers they did. But they also understood that when they were adults, things would be different for them than for their older sisters and brothers (or half sisters and brothers). They would experience most of their adult life without a father.

Charlotte is eleven. A precocious, sociable girl who has lots of friends, she lives with her mother and father, fifty-three and sixty-three years old, in a large house in San Francisco. Her father has three children from a previous marriage, ranging in age from thirty-five to forty-one, and three from this marriage, ranging from Charlotte at eleven to age twenty-three. Charlotte's next older sibling is nineteen.

"Most of my friends who know me know my father, but I know very few of their fathers," Charlotte tells us. "Their dads don't spend very much time with them. And when my friends are doing something important, their dads often don't come, but my father is always there. My father has had a lot of kids. He realizes what's important to us, and now he has a lot more time. At six o'clock he wants to be home instead of at work. My friends' fathers are working and they are at the start of their business careers — they're still aiming for that ten dollars an hour instead of eight. My dad works really hard and I respect that, but he doesn't have to push it to make that extra dollar so he can take us to Disneyland one more time. Neither of my parents are into the commercial kind stuff like Disneyland or Marine World. We go and play tennis or go for a bike ride or I take a walk with my dad and that is special for me. I like having the time with him."

She says that when her friends met her father they were kind of surprised at first at how old he was, but they didn't treat him differently. "I know a few people that when they found out that he was sixty-three, they were like, wow, he's like this old man," she says. "And I guess all my friends are surprised when they hear my mom and dad's ages. But then they get used to them, and they seem younger. It doesn't click in their minds that my dad is older. He has worked very hard to keep up his appearance. He bike rides almost every day and he gets a lot of exercise and he wants me to go with him. When you look at him, you don't guess he's sixty-three — you think late forties or early fifties. My friends are impressed at all the things he does with me. They say, 'He does that with you?' And there are things that I expect their fathers to do with them, like if we are talking about our parents at school or something, I'll be talking to them about what they did last weekend or whatever, and I'll say, you mean he didn't do that also? You mean that's all you did? I think that since my father has more time, I kind of expect that from their dads, and I realize that they don't spend that much time with their dads and they don't have a similar relationship at all."

Charlotte has another family image problem with her friends: the large age gap between her and her next older sibling. "My nineteen-year-old brother and twenty-three-year-old sister don't feel older when I'm with them," she says, "but compared to all my friends' brothers and sisters, they are a lot older than me. Most of my friends have brothers and sisters at most five or six years older, and my nearest brother is eight years older than me. When someone asks me how much older my oldest brother or sister is and I say twenty-nine years older, they think it's crazy. Well, you're eleven and he's twenty-nine years older, so what's your dad like?"

If she has to deal with comments like these, how does she feel when her father comes to school to pick her up? Is she embarrassed?

"It's not so much that the other kids feel strange or that they react when my parents come to school," she says. "But sometimes I feel awkward. When I see the other fathers with their hair gelled back, when they are wearing all the new modern things and my dad is still wearing his tweed coat, I am really aware of how he looks. I don't think anyone else sees it, but I do. I get over it, though. He is who he is."

And does she think at all about her father in the future? How it may be when she is an adult and he is not around? Does she worry about that?

"I don't really worry about losing my dad, but I think about that he might not be here when I'm twenty-six. I don't worry but I kind of wish he'll be around. My half brother Mark is forty-one now and he'll have him for another ten or twenty years. But my dad may not be around to help me through when I'm older. Mark is lucky for that. I don't worry about it that much, but sometimes when I'm lying in bed at night, I think, when I'm thirty-seven, Dad will be almost ninety, and I think, hmmm, he probably won't be here. My grandma only lived to eighty-nine.

"But I respect him that he's an older father and he made the choice to do that. There's nothing that he couldn't do because of his age but sometimes he doesn't want to do things, like just going to places because they're where everybody goes. He's not into a certain scene that a lot of my friends' parents are into. But I don't feel bad about that. That's just the type of person he is."

THE MORALITY OF MORTALITY

Kids worry about their older parents dying, and when they are older, some are angry that their parents left them too soon or were sick for a long time. With the responsibility and grief that illnesses in old age carry with them, it is not fun to have sick parents at any time in life, even in middle age when you are relatively well prepared to deal with issues of mortality. But as a teenager, it is a much more terrible burden to bear. It can turn childhood into an aberrant early adulthood. On those grounds, you would want to think carefully about the consequences of having children in your fifties and sixties.

Historically, though, parents' early sickness and death (and high infant mortality) has always been part of the human condition. Living much longer is only a recent phenomenon — as little as three generations young. The more positive features for children of older parenting are also a relatively recent phenomenon.

Contrary to popular opinion, we found that children see this difference positively—they think they are getting a better deal, not worse. This may be partly a condition of the times. Children of older parents today are more likely to be wanted children than accidents. Since these children have a sense of themselves that is more singular anyway, belonging to a small social category may not be detrimental. And in the communities where these children live, their older parents are a little less rare than they were ten years ago. The fact that there are even a few other children in a similar situation means that the off-spring of late parenting are not total "outsiders," allowing them to blend into some peer definition of normality.

Audrey, a fourteen-year-old whose seventy-two-year-old father, Michael, we met in the previous chapter, lives in a university town and knows three or four other teenagers with older dads—though maybe not as old as her father. "It makes things a little more normal," she says. "It makes it seem like less of a big deal that my father is older. Anyway, most of my sense of him is that the way he is has a lot less to do with his age than with the way he is as a person. My older half sister tells me he was that way when he was a younger dad too."

Our discussions with teenagers who have older parents suggested that although they do not worry that much about their fathers dying at any specific moment, they fear the void of a fatherless later life, in their twenties and thirties, as they pass through the experiences of adulthood.

For example, Audrey says, "I would just like to see my dad playing with my kids. But I doubt I will. It's pretty depressing to think about that. I do it when I'm feeling sorry for myself and want to feel like a martyr."

Teenagers also see their much older fathers as not able or wanting to do some of the things that kids like to do. Boys are particularly likely to be aware of their older fathers' more limited physical abilities, and the kinds of things they are willing or able to with the kids.

Are these issues important enough for society to raise such serious questions about older fathering? Is it a moral problem?

We do not think so. Children have no choice as to who their parents are, but when all is said and done, the absence of physical play or even a relatively early death cannot overwhelm the positive features of good fathering in childhood. If older fathers make good fathers in the formative years, that is the moral bottom line.

9

·   ·   ·   ·   ·   ·   ·   ·   ·   ·   ·   ·   ·   ·

Changes

The great advantage in the two of us, a generation apart, writing a book about older fathering is that we see the subject from very different perspectives. The father sees it from the point of view of a middle-aged man again going through the experience of fathering; the son sees it as a young adult both forced to deal with the consequences of his father's choice to become a father again — a choice over which he, the son, had no control — and the impending decision of whether and when to become a father himself.

The most obvious effect this had on our writing was that it helped us attain a certain middle ground. When the middle-aged father (Martin) was inclined to portray the late fathering experience in too rosy a light, the young adult son (David) would often paint a different reality. Likewise, when David was inclined to make cynical observations, Martin provided positive examples to counter David's negative view. The result, we hope, is a balanced, fairly objective picture of older fathering that shows several sides of the same issue.

But in addition to helping us achieve this middle ground, our generational differences gave us very different views of changes in families and fathering over the past thirty years. One of us originally fathered a family in the optimistic, socially active 1960s. The other gauges the prospects of family life in the 1990s with the more troubled eye of a generation facing the threat of AIDS, violence to children, and much lower economic possibilities.

Because we chose to present our findings using the collective "we," our different points of view did not appear overtly in the text. But it would be foolish for us to deny that such differences exist. Our readers are probably wondering whether we completely agreed on what we wrote and may be curious to know how our views differed. They also may be eager for us to personalize the subject further than we already have by putting ourselves directly into the picture. Would not that provide a whole other dimension to the book?

We agree, it would. We also feel that it would be important for the reader to hear our individual voices on some of the broader themes and questions we have presented along the way. That would be a means of personalizing these issues and providing insight into them. So here, in this last chapter, we drop our collective "we" and go our somewhat separate ways.

DO DODDERING DADS MAKE BETTER FATHERS?

MARTIN: Admittedly, it is not easy for me to sift through memories of family life almost thirty years old, but I do have the impression that raising a child in my fifties is a more intense and rewarding experience than it was then. Maybe everything takes more effort, so I am more aware of it. Maybe now I am more awed by childhood. Maybe feminism has changed my attitudes and sense of family. Maybe if I were a twenty-five-year-old father today, I would be into fathering about the same way I am at fifty-five. All that is possible. Yet, looking back on fathering you and your brother Jon in my twenties, I can remember certain things that make me think that I am a better father now than I was then.

For example, although I was very dedicated to both of you as progeny, I know that I was also hardly interested in you as small babies. I fulfilled my fatherly responsibilities: I changed diapers, fed you, and did all those things even in the mid 1960s. So I guess I was a "new father" before my time. But I also had traditional priorities, especially when you were young, and family usually lost out to work and, later, to my commitment to politics and social change. Most of the time, I didn't notice the incredible strides you made as babies and toddlers. I just wanted you to grow up as fast as possible so that we could play sports together or go on hikes — to be young adults together. I started you skiing early, put you in school early, and made you take responsibility for yourself early. I feel like I missed your babyhood. When I look back at your pictures from that time, I almost want to cry. I didn't realize how terrific you were, and how it was all going to be gone in a flash. That's probably the main reason I was willing to do it again.

I have a completely different view of babyhood this time around. I am acutely aware of how precious every day of Juliet's early years are. I'm not in any hurry to see her grow up. I am infinitely more patient. With you and Jon, when you misbehaved, I saw you as being too "childish" — you were invading my young adult space with your "crazy" behavior. With Juliet, I am happy to accept her as a child. Her behavior is not crazy; it's properly childish. I know that she has to learn to do things a "proper" way, but I also know that she will learn, all in good time. There is no rush.

This is the same message I got from most of the older fathers I interviewed. They all mentioned three things: as late fathers they had a heightened awareness of the infancy of their new child(ren); they spent a lot of time with their children because they felt an urgency not to miss their kids' childhood; and they were a lot more patient with their young children because they understood much more about how childhood evolved. The reasons are pretty obvious: We older dads now see the end of our lives much more clearly than we see back to our youth. We want to savor every moment, and that includes enjoying a young child. We also have a lot more confidence about ourselves as men. We know our possibilities and limitations, so we're not trying so much to prove to the world who we are. One of my interviewees said he thought that fathering was wasted on young men. They didn't have a clue and by the time they figured things out, it was too late. That's exactly how I feel about my own early fathering. My heart was in the right place, but I didn't have the experience or even the interest to learn about myself through you. I'm only thankful that you and Jon turned out the way you did.

DAVID: It's not easy for me to remember a lot of what happened all those years ago, either. I remember it as a sort of weird period — the late 1960s, early 1970s — there was a lot of strange stuff going on. I remember being six years old and running away from the police at an antiwar demonstration with you. And I remember people smoking dope at parties and going skinny-dipping.

As a family, we did a lot of things together, and we saw a lot of interesting events and places. We traveled a lot, and I'm grateful for all those experiences today. But I also remember a lot of yelling — you yelling at Jon and me, you yelling at our mother, her yelling back at you and at us, and me yelling back at all of you. You would always apologize after yelling, and I remember Jon saying right in the middle of one of your outbursts, "You might as well stop yelling right now because you're just going to feel bad about it later and apologize."

None of this stuff made you a bad father. The shouting was a small, negative side to your fathering in those early days, and I think you've come to terms with it as you've gotten to know yourself better and find your place in the world. And I know that you're not the only one to blame for the fights we had. I know our mother had her problems, too. She had her own set of issues to deal with. I will say this, though: You were fairly predictable. Your anger had its limits, and we knew that, which was comforting in a way. We knew you'd come to your senses sooner rather than later.

I suppose the main effect those years had on me is that I developed a bad temper in my teens. I still do have a bad temper, but I've learned to keep it in check. Fundamentally, I'm not an angry person, and I think that part of the reason I'm not is that I've come to realize (from you) how negative being angry can be. And as a result, I think I'll be a calmer parent than you were when you were younger. I think I'll be more like you are now as a parent.

In terms of the questions this book asks, I think the fathers who were good the first time around will also be good the second time around, and the ones who were not so good the first time may have become better, but they are a lot less terrific fathers the second time than they claim. They probably spend more time with their children, but they seem to be making many of the mistakes they made in the past. That includes repeating mistakes in their marriages.

My impression from the interviews I had with older fathers was that by the time a lot of these men's second or third marriages were ten years old, they were facing the same problems that their earlier ones went through after the same period of time. And the problems were affecting their children, just like the first set of children was affected in the previous round. I got another message: Most of the men did not necessarily marry for love, but for companionship. These men in their late forties or early fifties do not want to spend their late middle age alone—they needed to find someone.

Occasionally, I go to some upscale bars in New York and I see these men in their late forties looking for women. It's pretty depressing. I know that I don't want to be in that situation when I'm forty years old, still hanging out in a bar trying to meet a woman. I'm generalizing, but these are the type of men who don't really want kids, especially if they've had them before, but if that's what the woman they end up with wants, most of them would agree to go along. Having a child, with all its negatives, is better than being lonely.

MARTIN: I agree that our survey is not random, and it is self-selective because these men married younger women who wanted a child, whether their own or adopted. The men then turn around and report that having this child is just the greatest thing. Do you think that's not true? The older fathers really seem to enjoy having kids, seem to be more sensitive to them, and seem to be more willing to engage with them than younger fathers. All the academic studies with all their statistical controls show the same thing.

DAVID: Sure, the fathers feel that they are good fathers, and maybe they are. The ones we interviewed seemed to have a much calmer attitude and were spending a lot of quality time with their kids. They also were willing to be critical of themselves as younger fathers. But if we had asked them when they were in their twenties whether they were good fathers, would they have said, "I'm a bad father"?

The more I think about it, the more I think the key factor in this whole equation is whether they were good fathers—or at least had some talent for fathering—in the first place. If they were good fathers, I guess they are doing the right thing having more children—both for them and their new kids, and maybe even for their first kids. But if they don't have such a good track record, it is irresponsible for them to become fathers again.

MARTIN: There might be a Darwinian selection going on here that helps insure that the ones with the worst track records don't father again. You can't say much about whether a man in his early forties who has never had children is going to be a good father, but for the ones who had children before, you can always observe the relationship the father has with them. You interviewed the young woman who decided that she didn't really want to have children with her older husband when she got to know his kids from the first marriage. She realized that he had a bad track record, and it turned her off raising a family with him. Naturally, that meant that she would go out and look for someone else when the time came, so that marriage is probably doomed.

The woman does not even have to marry the man to figure that out. Usually, she meets the previous children sometime in their courtship—not necessarily, but usually. She should be able to tell pretty quickly what the relationship is with those kids. Jean didn't really want children—at least, that's what she said—but one of the reasons that she says she ended up wanting to have children with me is that she saw the close relationship I had with my previous children. It's the opposite case to the interview you did with that young woman who was not particularly interested in having children with her husband when she saw how messed up his children were. For Jean, what seemed like a good track record made her think that I would make a good person to parent with.

So in a way, a woman marrying an older man with fairly grown-up children has a better chance to tell about what kind of father he will make than if she marries a younger man who never fathered before. With the younger man, she simply imagines that since she loves him he must have the qualities that will make him a great father.

DAVID: The problem with your idea is that women and men are not that analytical when it comes to getting married or having children. They see what they want to see. A woman meets a divorced man, they are attracted to each other, and since they are both looking to get married, they soon think that they are in love. He tells her a story about what happened in his first marriage and that is the only story she hears. As far as his kids are concerned, she may not meet them until much later, and even if she does meet them, a lot of the true feelings that the children feel toward the father don't come out. Anyway, unless the kids are really messed up like they were in that one case, a lot of the problems with the father don't come out. A lot of kids apparently don't say anything about being sexually abused by the father until they are parents themselves and the father starts hanging around their kids—his grandchildren. But the bottom line is that unless there is something really bizarre between the father and the older kids, the woman pays a lot less attention to their relationship than the man's position in his job or his income. If he's got a good, stable position in life, and he seems all right genetically, that's what really counts for her. So I think the bad fathers are going to get a second chance to be poor fathers if they want to.

MARTIN: Don't forget those Late Bloomers in San Jose. There were a lot of them, and they thought the world of their older husbands. One said that she thought that her husband got better and better at fathering as he got older. What about on the personal side? Do you see a major difference between the way I fathered you guys and the way I father Juliet?

DAVID: It's very difficult for me to judge, because at this point she is only three years old, and I don't remember how it was when I was three years old. From what I do remember, you are calmer now. But you are an unusual example because you were always a good father. We were brought up with you. You were the one who took over when our mother left, so I'm always going to think of you as a good father who was there doing stuff for us. I honestly think Juliet is lucky to be in the situation she is in. She's got it better in one way for sure: We didn't have as many things as she does. I know that I didn't have thirty stuffed animals in my room. The other thing is that Jean is a good mother and is well prepared for motherhood. She comes from a big family, she has dealt with her sisters' children, a lot of her friends got married and had children, and she is an elementary school teacher, so she knows a lot about dealing with children. Would I like to grow up under these circumstances? I guess the answer is yes. I think Juliet has a very good life. But it's really not that different from my life as a child, no matter how bad you may want to make it seem in your own mind. It's funny that I have a better image of your fathering us than you do.

WHICH IS WORSE: DIVORCE OR DEATH?

DAVID: I think you were having a lot of problems figuring out whether you really wanted to have a family when you were in your mid twenties. I can understand that because I'm about that age now and have some of the same feelings, but I didn't get married and have kids. You were dealing with young adulthood—the transition that Levinson talks about—and you were under a lot of stress with it. My sense, understanding you at that age from the way I feel now, is that in a lot of ways there were parts of you that did not want to be tied down. You hadn't sowed your oats, and that had an effect on your relationship with my mother. I personally believe that even if someone falls deeply in love, he should feel really ready to settle down before he gets married and has kids. It's hard for me to imagine that I would do that at twenty-two or twenty-three the way you did. Maybe the fact that you could afford it and that all your friends were getting married pushed you to think that you should do it, too. But if you aren't ready, it almost guarantees divorce. Whether you are a more or less involved father has a lot smaller effect on your children than divorce. I remember you as an active father even if you don't see yourself that way. But your divorce had a really big impact on my life. Your fatherhood to me will always be set in terms of that event. That's the big negative of getting married so young, and probably the biggest positive of being the child of older parents—they probably won't get divorced.

MARTIN: You're right about that. My knowledge about husband-wife relations probably increased even more than about children in the last twenty years. It's certain that an older man knows himself a lot better, but that does not mean that he makes a better husband—at least that's what we seemed to find in our interviews. The chances of divorce in families when there is a reasonable age difference and the husband is in his forties or early fifties is lower than when people marry in their twenties. You are right about my confusion when I was in my twenties, but I never thought that our marriage would end. My parents, your mother's parents, and all their friends were married once and forever. It caught me totally by surprise. The amazing thing is how many of the children born in the 1960s and 1970s went through it. Now it's almost normal that your parents get divorced and you are raised by one parent—mainly your mother. When you see that happening and realize how painful it is for the kids, you easily conclude that new fathering versus traditional fathering styles or time involvement within a family where the parents get along reasonably may not be the most important issue in town. So the real case for older fathering may be in reduced divorce rates rather than in the more intense attention the father pays to the children or his sensitivity to his young children's day-to-day needs. If older families are more likely to stick together, then it may also overcome the fact that older fathers are not going to be as athletic with their sons, and are going to embarrass their kids when they show up at school events. That's probably exaggerated anyway.

DAVID: I guess you would try to weigh the drawbacks of having an older father who is not athletic and is tired a lot of the time against the drawbacks of having a father who is active but has the problems of going through that transitional period of the late twenties and early thirties. Weighing the two, I'm not sure how I would come out. I guess I would rather have a younger father who could play sports with me, but is that worth having a father going through a divorce in his thirties, going through the stress of that, and trying to figure out who he is and his place in the world? I would say that it's a tough choice.

MARTIN: There is this other aspect, though. Older fathers like me have a higher probability of dying early. Which is worse, divorce or death? At least the divorced father is still around. You will very likely have your mother and father around when you are in your forties and fifties. If you were this age now and your father had died already, don't you think it would affect your life in a negative way?

DAVID: Yes, it would be bad, and I can see that it will affect Juliet's life a lot if you die in her mid twenties. She is obviously going to be very close to you. But at the same time, people deal with what they are dealt in life. Everyone, from time to time, and to various degrees, would rather be someone else. Many people are born into very bad situations and some do very well.

Obviously, from my point of view, I would rather have gone through what I went through with your divorce than to have you die. But Juliet probably isn't going to have that choice. Even so, at least she'll be aware there's a good chance you're going to die when she is relatively young, and she'll deal with it. The fact that she has such a good relationship with you and that you spend so much time with her, it's going to make it hard on her, but it will also prepare her better for being without you. And she will still have her mother, and lots of family on her mother's side, and, of course, me and Jon.

FATHERING OLD AND FATHERING YOUNG IN THE 1990S

MARTIN: I don't have a sense of when and how I would become a father if I were twenty-five or thirty years old today. I guess it must be very different, because young people with college education are waiting a lot longer to have families. From what I have read and seen, making the decision to raise children in today's economic and social environment is not easy. If you think about it very much, it probably doesn't happen. Maybe the only way to do it is to go into a relationship, take chances, and then pay the consequences. How do you view getting married and fathering? Especially after all these interviews?

DAVID: I think you're right. I see people my age choosing to play more and put off having children. They don't take it as lightly as they used to. I don't know whether it's because of divorce, but most people I know see having kids as very serious—a big responsibility. At the same time, there are still a lot of people who are getting married and having kids in their twenties. It seems to be divided more by social class than when you got married in the early 1960s. High school–educated people get married earlier and college-educated men get married much later.

On the other hand, things have not changed that much from the time you were getting divorced in the 1970s. A lot of women who are in their early to mid thirties and have young children are getting divorced.

I guess the question is how many of my peers in their late twenties are getting married. My sense is that it depends on what sort of family background you came from. If you came from a family where the parents had children relatively early, and they stayed together all these years and had this nice, stable structure, I think the son of the family is more likely to see that as his model and to see having children more in terms of timing. Okay, I am twenty to thirty years old, I've just gotten married, my wife wants to have kids because it is about time for her. It's timing. I'll give you an example. I have a friend out on the West Coast who was going out with a woman for four or five years, then broke up with her, and began living with another woman. Within a few months this second woman got pregnant. The way my friend explained it me, one day they were just talking and she mentioned that the doctors had told her she could not have children because of some childhood condition, so she did not know if she could ever have a child. He said, "I've never tried to have a kid." It was like a challenge. They tried, and sure enough, she got pregnant. I called his answering machine one day and I got a message that he was on his honeymoon. This thing had begun as an experiment, and now he was married and his wife was expecting a child. It seemed bizarre. On his twenty-eighth birthday, my friend had wished for a family. So he got his family, but the child was born premature, there were tremendous medical bills, and now they have this child with all the responsibilities that go along with it. He works at home, so he is there a lot, and the wife also stays home to take care of the kid. His life is kind of where he wants it to be right now, but he is going to have some troubles in the future. He told me, "I didn't realize it at the time, but I found the perfect woman to marry." Well, if he didn't realize it at the time, who knows what is going to happen. He only met her six months before she got pregnant and they were married within less than a year. I don't think this is as unusual a story as it seems, and maybe that's why these young families have such a high divorce rate.

MARTIN: Is this story an anomaly, or do guys your age or younger who are college educated still want to have kids? This is important in trying to understand what the future is going to look like in terms of younger and older fathers.

DAVID: Yes, we still want to have families, but not necessarily when we are young. My friend's story is not that unusual, but it shows that you almost have to stop thinking to do it sooner rather than later. If you put any thought into it, you wait until you are in your early or mid thirties. I think I'll see a lot more of my friends in the next three or four years getting married. Before, people got married right out of college. In my class, only a handful did. I think that has to do with people not getting as rich as fast. And when you hear all these statistics on divorce, you think twice about marriage. It's pretty simple to understand that one of two marriages ends in divorce. So you want to be pretty sure that you are going to settle down with someone you know well and want to stay with. You also have to be more sure you know yourself.

MARTIN: The most important factor seems to be that women are working more now — that they are more career oriented, so they wait to get married and have children. Some wait so long that they get into fertility trouble and then think that they made a big mistake.

DAVID: Women are working more too and are more career oriented, but at a certain moment — like when they are about thirty — they are willing to stop for a few years to have kids. My impression is that there are very few women who are so career oriented that they are willing to wait until their late thirties or even their mid thirties to think about having children. I've seen that women want to settle down by the time they are thirty, even if they've made some money and established a track record in the labor market. Most women I know have always really wanted to have a family and they know they need to get going on that by their late twenties, early thirties. They need to meet Mr. Right by that time. Why? Because let's say they meet him when they are thirty. They go out with him for a year, get married, then they have another year or two to enjoy being married without children, which already puts them at thirty-three or thirty-four. That's the timetable they're looking at.

However, I see one problem interfering with this timetable: It is becoming more and more difficult for thirty-year-old women to find men of the same age who are willing to commit to marriage. That explains why they end up marrying older men, like my friend Beth, who is thirty-two and finally met a guy who is forty. He was looking to get married and she was looking to get married. About a year ago, she told me, "I want to be in love and married." That's what she wanted, which is a dangerous thing on a certain level, and she moved in with this guy six weeks after meeting him. They haven't gotten married yet, but I assume they will. And so he is going to be a somewhat older father.

Another attractive and smart thirty-year-old woman I know was also looking to get married, and she also had trouble finding someone around her age. She is now living with a guy who is forty-seven, and they are probably going to get married. He has a kid and they're going to have kids. I told her that forty-seven is pretty old, and she said, "Oh, he's very young at heart." My feeling is that when you're out there looking for a prospective spouse and you find someone you think is a desirable candidate, you look beyond the flaws. When he has three-fourths of what you are looking for, you forget the drawbacks.

MARTIN: I think you are much better prepared to have children than I was. I was not at all aware of what to do as a father. I started reading books when you and Jon were teenagers. I couldn't figure out what was going on, and I started reading books and I said, "Hey! They are behaving exactly like the book says." It made me feel a lot better. I should have done it a lot earlier.

DAVID: Now that I have seen you and read some of the books about fathering so that I could write about it, I can see how little my friends know about children and parenting; my friends are all college graduates but still are almost totally unprepared to be parents. I get the impression that little has changed that way. When I was growing up I had a friend in the neighborhood who was sent to a military school, and I always wondered why he had such problems as a child—he used to throw plates at his mother and stuff like that. I assumed that he was just a troubled kid, but years later I talked to his father at a wedding and I asked him if he had really sent the boy away to a military school. He said yes, it was true, and he admitted that he really knew nothing about fathering. The children came along, and he just "did" fathering. He did not understand the first thing about child-rearing. The parents seemed reasonable enough—professional people—but then years later, you learn that they didn't know anything about parenting. It's kind of shocking. I feel, after writing this book, that I know quite a bit about fathering. There is a certain point when you really want to become a father, and the more you know, probably the later that point is.

MARTIN: From what you are saying and my observations as an economist, it seems that the more education in the population, the longer young people are going to wait to parent, and that may be a very good thing both for them and for their kids. The number of middle-aged fathers may also keep increasing, even when the baby boomer effect plays out in about ten to fifteen years, because of what you said about these thirty- to thirty-five-year-old women having difficulty finding men their own age to marry, so turning to older men. This assumes that the older men are going to feel that they can afford to have children at that age. Incomes for the forty-five- to fifty-four-year-old age group are dropping so fast that ten years from now, there may not be that many middle-aged men who feel they can afford to father again in their mid forties. I can tell you that it is really scary to have the additional expenses at my age because I am already worried what might happen to my family if I get sick or die, or what my retirement might be like if I'm not able to save enough money. I never thought this way when I was young.

DAVID: But you did it anyway. That's what I have been saying. I think people make decisions because of what they feel they should be doing in life at that particular moment. A lot of people asked me why I thought you'd gone ahead and had this child when you were already in your fifties. The easiest answer was that your wife wanted to have a child and that you had simply capitulated. But I never felt that was entirely true. I always thought you just said that to deflect some of the responsibility away from you. My impression was that, deep down, you wanted this child from the start — or at least, you were vulnerable to the idea of having a child. Why? For two reasons: First, you've always liked children and always wished you had more. And second, you were having or approaching a midlife crisis and liked the idea of starting over and returning to something you did in your youth.

There's nothing wrong with that. In fact, one of the positive things I see about your having a child again is that it lets you express yourself in a way that makes you feel young. The irony is that your having a child has also given me a window into my past. Watching you be a father to Juliet has made me think about what it was like for me when I was growing up. I can imagine myself being Juliet and kind of remembering how it was when I was just a little older than she is. So I get to see you being my father. But I get to see it from an adult's perspective, which is pretty amazing if you stop to think about it. It's sort of like watching a home movie and being in it at the same time. It's very illuminating. Of course, now that I have been working on this book, I am much more aware of the problems associated with fathering and child development. But watching you has made me realize how ready you have to be to change your lifestyle totally when you have children. Your children become the center of attention. The freedom is gone. You obviously have to be ready to put yourself in that position, whatever age you are.

*

During the months we worked on this project, the question most often asked of us was what it was like to write a book together as father and son. It was interesting to watch people's faces as we gave our answers, because many of them seemed to be trying to imagine what it would be like to write a book with their fathers or sons. Most said that they could not imagine it. "Not a chance," one man said. "We would have disowned each other before we finished the introduction."

For us, writing together was easy, almost natural. Did we know it would be like that from the very beginning? No, not really. Martin was worried that David would not be "into" the project because it was Martin's idea. He may have had good reason. The truth is that David had doubts at first. But then, as we began to conduct the interviews and listen to people's stories, David realized that this was much richer material than he had expected, and that the issues we were dealing with were actually very complex. They were not only complex for Martin's generation, but affected David as a potential first-time father.

Before we sat down to write, we wanted to get a firm idea of what the goals of the book would be. We quickly realized that our book was not going to make our readers' decision to become a father in late middle age, or to mother a child with an older father, any easier. Nor would we make those older fathers who wake up thinking that they are in an episode of "The Twilight Zone" feel any more sane about the decision they have already made. But what we could do was help our audience understand what it has meant for other people to be older fathers and put their experience in a social context.

What we did not anticipate was how it would affect our own relationship. In writing our first-person introductions and giving our separate responses in this chapter, we were forced to have discussions and say things to each other we probably would not have otherwise. These exchanges have not necessarily made us feel any closer (because we were close before we began writing), but they have certainly given us a better understanding of where each of us stands and how we feel about certain events that not only relate to us but to our family as a whole. It showed us that the rediscovery of fathering with a new child can, if you allow it to, also deepen the fathering experience in other directions.

Our greatest hope is that our discussions will encourage you, the readers, to reflect on some of the same questions that we have considered (and others we may have missed), and that you will come to a similarly enriched understanding of yourself and your families. One of the nice things that's happening for middle-aged men and women is that society's conception of how they are supposed to spend those "quiet" retirement years is changing. Fathering (and mothering) may become among the few occupations that you can do anytime in your life, better later than earlier, perhaps, and always improving as you go along.

Notes

CHAPTER 2 NOTES

1. Nikki Meredith, "Dear Old Dad: Can Wisdom and Time Make Up for Lost Energy?" Chicago *Tribune*, February 28, 1988, p. 8.

2. Andrew Yarrow, *Latecomers* (New York: Free Press, 1991).

3. Pamela Daniels and Kathy Weingarten, "The Fatherhood Click: The Timing of Parenthood in Men's Lives," in P. Bronstein and C. P. Cown, eds., *Fatherhood Today* (New York: John Wiley, 1988); pp. 36–52. This article is a continuation of their work in *Sooner or Later: The Timing of Parenthood in Adult Lives* (New York: Norton, 1982).

4. See for example, Corinne N. Nydegger, Linda S. Mitteness, and John O'Neil, "Experiencing Social Generations," *Research on Aging*, vol. 5, no. 4 (December, 1983); pp. 527–46. See also Corinne N. Nydegger, "The Development of Paternal and Filial Maturity," in Karl Pillemer and Kathleen McCartney, eds., *Parent-Child Relations Throughout Life* (Hillsdale, N.J.: Erlbaum, 1991). Nydegger's Fatherhood Project focused on father-adult child relations among 267 well-educated middle-class men in the San Francisco Bay area and 104 of their children—62 sons and 62 daughters.

5. Ross D. Parke and Brian Neville, "Late Time Fatherhood: Determinants and Consequences for Children and Families," in Jerrold Lee Shapiro, Michael J. Diamond, and Martin Greenberg, eds., *Becoming a Father: Contemporary Perspectives* (New York: Springer Publishing, forthcoming).

6. Gail Sheehy, *Passages* (New York: E. P. Dutton, 1976).

7. Daniel J. Levinson with Charlotte Darrow, Edward Klein, Maria Levinson, and Braxton McKee, *The Seasons of a Man's Life* (New York: Alfred A. Knopf, 1978).

8. Ibid., p. 62.

9. Ibid., p.107.

10. Betty Friedan, *The Second Stage* (New York: Summit Books, 1981), p. 137, quoted in Robert Griswold, *Fatherhood in America* (New York: Basic Books, 1993), p. 246.

11. Griswold, *Fatherhood in America*.

12. Until the mid 1970s, the first phase of this influx of married women into the workplace was mainly the result of increased demand for low-cost labor, smaller families, and women's rising aspirations for financial and social independence from their husbands. The second phase was quite different. After 1973, men's real earnings began to decline, compelling even those married women who would have preferred staying out of the labor market to seek jobs. Between 1973 and 1993, men's weekly earnings adjusted for inflation fell more than 14 percent, which meant that wives had to go out and work just to help the family break even.

13. Historian Robert Griswold explains it this way in his book *Fatherhood in America*: "Inspired by feminist theory, critical of the increasing bureaucratization and routinization of work, and cognizant of changing gender relationships in general, men in the early 1970s began formulating a critique of traditional masculinity and made some of the earliest calls for a new, politically informed fatherhood. The liberal, ostensibly feminist perspective averred that traditional manhood and fatherhood were a kind of prison, a set of 'roles' with unrealistic expectations that led men to do bad things and put them out of touch with their 'real,' more nurturing selves" (p. 247).

14. Griswold, *Fatherhood in America*, p. 227. Other studies cited by Griswold found that men could be performing various tasks around the house, but most did not take such responsibility, and found that fathers in two-worker families were much less engaged with their children than were mothers, were less accessible, and took responsibility for child care only about 10 percent of the time.

15. See Jerrold Lee Shapiro, *The Measure of a Man* (New York: Delacorte Press, 1993).

16. Griswold, *Fatherhood in America*, p. 229.

17. See note 2, above.

18. For a work that focuses mainly on the relationship between adult women and their fathers, see Suzanne Fields, *Like Father, Like Daughter* (Boston: Little, Brown, 1983).

CHAPTER 3 NOTES

1. *New York Times*, August 23, 1990.

2. Marilyn Elias, "Make Room for Baby," *USA Today*, August 19, 1993, p. 1D.

3. Jerrold Lee Shapiro, *The Measure of a Man*, p. 123.

CHAPTER 5 NOTES

1. Independent adoptions through attorneys did exist, even a generation ago, but were much rarer than today.

2. The agencies' position was logical. They saw their role in matching children to suitable, "normal" parents as "in the best interest" of a mother turning her child over to someone else's upbringing.

3. There are a number of good books about open adoption, including

Lois Ruskai and Sharon Kaplan Roszia, *The Open Adoption Experience* (San Antonio, TX: Corona, 1993); Jeanne W. Lindsay, *Open Adoption: A Caring Option* (New York: Harper, 1988); and James L. Gritter, *Adoption Without Fear* (Buena Park, CA: Morning Glory Press, 1989).

4. "All Things Considered," June 13, 1994.

5. Paul Tick, "Ambivalence About Adoption," *Genesis 2,* Winter 1987–88 (Cambridge, Mass.), p. 22.

CHAPTER 7 NOTES

1. The median age of mothers having their first child hit a post-1940 low of 21.8 years in 1960 (see U.S. Department of Health and Human Services, *Vital Statistics of the United States, 1988, Volume I–Natality* (National Center for Health Statistics, Hyattsville, Md. 1992), Table 1–11.

2. Levinson et al., *The Seasons of a Man's Life,* p. 49. Italics in original.

3. Ibid. p. 48.

4. The divorce rate per thousand married women shot up beginning in the late 1960s, rising to levels higher than at any time since 1945–47, when the men came home from World War II. This was not a Vietnam effect, since the rates continued to rise into the early 1980s. The numbers look like this:

Year	Divorce Rate per 1,000 Married Women 15 Years Old & Older
1920	8.0
1930	7.5
1940	8.8
1945	14.4
1946	17.9
1947	13.6
1950	10.3
1955	9.3
1960	9.2
1965	10.6
1970	14.9
1975	20.3
1980	22.6
1985	21.7
1987	20.8

Source: U.S. Department of Health and Human Services, *Vital Statistics of the United States, 1988, Volume III–Marriage and Divorce,* Table 2–1.

Divorce also occurred earlier. The average age of divorce from the first marriage dropped as the marriage age fell. In the late 1960s and early 1970s, the divorce rate rose and divorce age simultaneously fell to the late twenties for women and to about thirty years old for men.

5. Griswold, *Fatherhood in America.*

6. Statistical Handbook on the American Family, Table C1–8.

7. The percentage of young black men who had attended and completed college in the 1949 labor force was much lower, at 5 and 3 percent respectively. Their incomes were much lower, too.

8. We have shown all these incomes only for white men. Because of affirmative action, black male college graduates who were in their late twenties in 1969 did much better than the corresponding age group of whites, catching up quickly to white incomes in the early 1970s and up to 1979. That gain continued in the 1980s, as these "tried and true" black men attained higher professional positions in their forties. They did enormously better than the black college graduates who were twenty-nine in 1959 and had entered the labor market in the 1950s when opportunities for black professionals were really limited. The group that came into the labor market a decade later also did well. The 1979 twenty-nine-year-olds started out at about the same income level and also made large gains in their thirties. By 1989, the twenty-nine-year-old black college graduates of 1979 (thirty-nine-year-olds in 1989) had caught up even closer to whites. However, the black male college graduates twenty-nine years old in 1989 started out at a much lower level of income than either the 1969 or 1979 twenty-nine-year olds. The Reagan Administration's move away from enforcing affirmative action in labor markets eventually hit hardest the young black male college graduates who had most profited from it. To read more about this, see Martin Carnoy, *Faded Dreams: The Politics and Economics of Race in America* (New York: Cambridge University Press, 1994).

9. There are a couple of interesting things to note about this trend pertaining to fathering young children after forty-five years old. When we look at historical statistics on birth rates by age and race of father, we see that in 1940, the birth rate for fathers of all races, forty-five to forty-nine years old, was high—about 18 per thousand men in that age group for whites and 35 per thousand for nonwhites. In 1940, the high numbers resulted from the combined effect of starting families later and from the tendency to have larger families. The numbers stayed high until after the early 1960s, when those who were in the forty-five- to forty-nine-year-old age group had begun getting married earlier (back in the 1940s) and having smaller families. The same happened to whites and nonwhites. By 1978, the rates had hit bottom, at 5 per thousand among whites and 13 per thousand among nonwhites. Nonwhites continued to begin having children younger and having larger families. By 1989, the rates had risen again for both groups, to 6.3 for whites and 14.6 for nonwhites, in this case mainly because of the effect of higher-educated couples postponing having children. The *Statistical Handbook on the American Family* (fig. D2–2) shows that until 1960, about 17 percent of married couples where the husband was forty-five to forty-nine years old had children under six years old in the household. This dropped to about 5 percent of couples who had young children by 1980, mainly because families finished having children much earlier.

10. *USA Today*, September 22, 1993, p. 6A.

11. The Families and Work Institute is an independent research institute. James Levine quoted in John Ritter, "As 'Mr. Moms,' More Dads No Longer Miss Out," *USA Today*, September 22, 1993, p. 6A.

12. Jerrold Lee Shapiro, *The Measure of a Man*. Italics in original.

CHAPTER 8 NOTES

1. Andrew Yarrow, *Latecomers,* p. 123.

2. Richard Griffen, "From Sacred to Secular: Memoir of a Mid-Life Transition Toward Spiritual Freedom," in L. Eugene Thomas and Susan Eisenhandler, eds., *Aging and the Religious Dimension* (Westport, Conn.: Auburn House, 1994); pp.31–50.

3. Ibid., p. 41.

4. Yarrow, *Latecomers,* p. 60.

5. Ibid., p. 61.

6. Ibid., pp. 60–61.

7. Ibid., p. 76.

8. Ibid., p. 97.

9. Arlene Levinson, "Older Parents: Often a Blessing for Kids; Families: As More Couples Delay Parenthood, More Children Find a Special Kind of Security Blanket," *Los Angeles Times,* June 28, 1991, E9.

10. On the other hand, the chance of a fifty-year-old father living until age seventy-five is close to 60 percent, so it is really the chance of living past seventy-five that is much lower.